PRAISE FOR JARROD McGRATH

'I have absolutely no doubt that Jarrod McGrath is one of the global leaders in the space of workforce management. His book *The Digital Workforce* is a vital read for leaders of any organisation, but particularly those coming to terms with having a digital workforce. Contemporary, thought provoking and absolutely essential reading in every way.'

– *Andrew Griffiths, International bestselling Author, Global Speaker and Entrepreneurial Futurist*

'Remarkable people are at the heart of every organisation. Magical things happen when people are inspired. *The Digital Workforce* shines a spotlight on how to fully embrace people by leveraging technology.'

– *Aron Ain, CEO of UKG (Ultimate Kronos Group) and author of* WorkInspired: How to Build an Organization Where Everyone Loves to Work

'Jarrod is always looking for what is next, what can I improve, how can I help organisations and leaders improve. This book really illustrates Jarrod's quest for knowledge coupled with making organisations thrive.'

– *Georgegina Poulos, Global Director People T2 and Global Retail Operations at Unilever*

'I commend Jarrod on his journey to keep the workforce current with the demands mandated by digital transformation. Congratulations on the second edition of the book with practical insights on how businesses can change their operating models in a human-centred way to incorporate people, algorithms and the broader environment.'

– *Matt Michalewicz, CEO, Complexica*

'Before I met Jarrod McGrath, I had only a very limited understanding of the term "workforce management". Since getting to know Jarrod and reading his book, I've realised that, done correctly, workforce management is an integral part of human capital management and touches just about every part of a business. *The Digital Workforce* is a must-read for anyone in business who seeks to truly understand the inter-relatedness of workforce management, the rise of the digital workforce and the evolution of this important field.'

– Cian McLoughlin, CEO and Founder at Trinity Perspectives

'At a time when industrial relations practices are being rewritten not only due to the digital transformation of workforces, but also due to the exposure of unacceptable behaviour such as wage theft and discrimination, Jarrod offers very timely insights and methodologies to ensure the workplace is a positive and profitable environment.'

– Hannah Watterson, Director and Public Relations Doyen, Watterson Marketing Communications

'Jarrod makes it so obvious every business needs to focus on a digital workforce strategy to really succeed. For me, the real-world examples make it real and useful.'

– Kim Benito, General Manager, Client Services, NTT DATA Business Solutions Australia

To my family – Michelle, Molly, Tadhg and Billie-Mae –
for letting me do what I love so much.

To the team at Smart WFM, for supporting my vision of
empowering people and organisations to achieve greater value.
Thank you for your dedication and for constantly raising the bar
to continually deliver great experiences for our customers
in a rapidly changing world.

To our clients and partners, for trusting us to advise,
implement and deploy people-related initiatives
in your organisations.

'Those with the vision to focus on digital transformation will empower their people to achieve more, personally and professionally.We have moved beyond shareholder return to a world that balances the needs of stakeholders across people, technology and the environment.'

Jarrod McGrath

More than 80 per cent of business leaders plan to accelerate their workforce digitisation post-pandemic.[1] But having a plan is one thing; taking the right action is another.

This book provides practical insights and actionable advice to help you utilise technology to manage your workforce effectively. The result: happier, healthier employees and a brighter, more prosperous future for your organisation.

---

1   World Economic Forum 2020, *The Future of Jobs Report*, weforum.org/reports/
    the-future-of-jobs-report-2020.

Project management and text design by Publish Central
Cover design by Peter Reardon

CONTENTS

FOREWORD

Today, more than ever, we continue to learn that our world can change literally overnight. In 2020 we learned that our ability to adapt and respond to change is truly the most important trait we can have in operating our business as well as our lives. The ability to digitally manage the workforce is more important than ever. As we all work together to create our next 'NOW' of work, our ability to digitise our organisation will offer the largest competitive advantage around the world.

The concept of capturing a worker's time and paying them accordingly is nothing new. We have been working hard over the past century to accurately compensate individuals for the work they do. In a manufacturing economy this was tough enough, and was based on an individual showing up for work, documenting their attendance and processing their pay. The ability to do this has been a mainly manual effort and one that is prone to error as well as filled with manual heroics to simply ensure that the workforce gets paid. Well, the future of the workforce combined with the process of managing it has become much more complex, creating the need for our function to be more agile than ever. Welcome to the world of the 'digital workforce'.

In the second edition of *The Digital Workforce*, Jarrod documents the journey we have been on for the past century from the second Industrial Revolution of the assembly line to where we are today in the middle of the fourth Industrial Revolution; a world that is filled with a post-2020 uncertainty and filled with new technologies begging to assist in automation including artificial intelligence and machine learning. Now, more than ever, our role will be vital in working to shift from capturing time and processing pay to an empathetic leadership role that uses our head and our heart to understand our workforce and to forecast, predict and provide business with tools not imagined until recently. This shift involves so much more than just technology; it is true transformation that touches the core of the business and creates a set of intelligence that will make or break the future of an organisation.

The Digital Workforce teaches us the important lessons on how true workforce management can solve problems. It provides an important lens through which all in HR and payroll and other lines of business can look to not just understand but mandate a new focus on the area of workforce management. Jarrod does a brilliant job of detailing the key areas that workforce management impacts in a business by thoroughly documenting the outcomes true workforce management can provide. All organisations worldwide are constantly looking to show the return on investment (ROI) of their initiatives and, through Jarrod's work on documenting the problems that workforce management can solve, we now have the toolkit we need to show not only ROI but true VOI (value of our investment) from our advanced and enhanced practices.

We all have learned in this industry that proving and showing value is one thing but taking action is another. In a world that is so fragile, we are asked to be agile while keeping costs in mind. We must learn to play offense and defence together and continue to show value while transforming. *The Digital Workforce* not only helps us with value, it details the step-by-step processes required to achieve ultimate success. In order to achieve success, this book walks us through a five-step process that discusses alignment to preparation; from implementation to tracking our results; and finally it teaches us how to not only 'go live' but truly measure the impact of our efforts. This five-step process has become and will continue to be the authoritative approach on how to lead any workforce management initiative. In each step of this SMART process, *The Digital Workforce* gives us examples, learnings, actions and takeaways that are 'musts' in our workforce management initiatives. The other invaluable way Jarrod documents this process is through the examples he provides, ranging from industry to type of workforce being managed to the different technological solutions to achieve results. Again, providing value is one thing, but providing the proof is another and Jarrod has done this with great success.

The successful deployment of workforce management as a practice requires a careful blend of people, process and technology while keeping our workforce at the centre, our workforce that takes a 'whole person' approach. *The Digital Workforce* does a comprehensive job of combining these concepts and sharing examples and requirements of the people and audiences needed to be reached, the processes and journeys that need to be digitised and 'reimagined', and finally Jarrod goes into depth discussing the technologies available today and into the future and what the impact of artificial intelligence and robotics will be on our industry.

This updated version of *The Digital Workforce* continues to be the leading resource for the industry to move from concept to context in the world of workforce management in truly providing success. It is a must-read for anyone looking to capture the value of their workforce from a business impact point of view, as well as for all of us looking to make our industry one that shifts from transactional to strategic. As someone who has spent their career in the HR and workforce technology industry, working with leaders around the world creating strategies and actions in alignment with their visions, I truly appreciate how hard this work is and the effort that goes into it. The fact that Jarrod has documented and UPDATED these efforts for the Now of Work in a manner that is easy to comprehend gives us a tool as an industry that will continue to create value and educate us all, even in these times of change.

Congratulations on this latest version Jarrod and be proud, you are changing the industry we are proud to be part of and I know your readers will appreciate it as much as I do.

Jason Averbook
CEO, Leapgen

ABOUT THE AUTHOR

Jarrod McGrath is a people and technology expert, visionary leader, future thinker, public speaker, media commentator, industry pioneer and author. As the founder and CEO of Smart WFM (smartwfm.com), he knows what organisations need to prosper in the modern world where digital is normal.

Jarrod grew up in the small country town of Bathurst, New South Wales, Australia. Bathurst is famous for three things: farming, motor car racing and education. As a young bloke riding motorbikes around on farms, it became obvious to Jarrod that agriculture was not his calling. He fell in love with cars, especially fast ones, which is still a passion of his – but it's not the topic of this book!

Jarrod has always been an entrepreneur. At the age of 10 he started his first word processing business. At 14 he established his own discotheque business, which he owned and operated for 10 years. Even in the early days, Jarrod's entire music collection was digitised with databases for his customers to choose their preferred music.

In 1999 Jarrod established one of the world's first 100 per cent online internet art auction sites. He later sold this, and founded a 100 per cent online art analytics business, which made historical art auction results available via the internet to help investors inform their buying decisions.

From the early 2000s Jarrod founded and worked in two dedicated people-related businesses. Jarrod loves being in the people business; providing opportunities for and growing people is a great interest of his.

Jarrod studied the theory of workforce management (WFM), operations research and artificial intelligence (AI) at university. From the outset, he was intrigued to understand how a business could run more effectively and deliver greater value by using its human and non human resources optimally.

Jarrod has been responsible for, and successfully delivered, literally hundreds of WFM programs to clients across a multitude of industries including retail, health, construction, manufacturing, hospitality, service and government. His expertise is in both local and international sales and delivery for large and small-to-medium-sized clients, solving an amazing number of interesting and valuable people-related business problems.

A regular media commentator, Jarrod's thought leadership has been featured in The Mandarin, *The Australian Financial Review*, *The Australian*, HRM, *CEO Magazine* and more.

> Jarrod McGrath is passionate about promoting the importance and value of people in the digital workplace. He is a skilled and energetic public speaker. For further information and to find out about Jarrod's availability, please contact: **speaking@smartwfm.com**.

A LOT HAS CHANGED IN RECENT YEARS

Workforce management (WFM) utilises methods of managing people more efficiently. It improves productivity; provides financial acuity, purpose and inspiration; builds brand loyalty; and empowers a digital workforce using all the technologies that we are spoiled with in the modern world.

WFM dates back to the 1890s, and its evolution has been closely aligned with revolution – industrial revolution, that is. Few people realise there have actually been four industrial revolutions – the latest of which we are in right now.

When I released the first edition of *The Digital Workforce* I had recently read *The Fourth Industrial Revolution* by Klaus Schwab, Founder and Executive Chairman of the World Economic Forum. I was fascinated by his insights into the exponential growth of technology and the confluence of technologies such as artificial intelligence (AI), robotics, the Internet of Things (IoT), 3D printing and so on. The influence of technology is spread across nations, governments, economies, businesses and communities. The speed at which these technologies are impacting people and organisations is greater than ever before – particularly with the onset of COVID-19. Organisations and their workforces are being reshaped, realigned and re-tooled, as well as being challenged to ensure a human-centred (rather than dehumanising) approach to work processes.

The parallels between the history of WFM and the industrial revolutions are around the significance of the developments and our ability to adopt, adapt to and embrace them in a thoroughly ubiquitous way. Each of the industrial revolutions resulted in modernisation and transformation: moving from farms to cities, the emergence of the skilled worker; the invention of steam engines; the introduction of the assembly line; the advent of electricity; the development of the microprocessor; and machine learning, to name a few.

Over time, WFM has evolved from initially being a system of record, to a system of productivity, to a system creating a unique workforce experience – bringing both the employer and employee closer together through empowerment and collaboration.

Organisations today are fortunate in that they no longer have to accept things as being just 'the way they are'. Digital technologies – mobile devices, social media, algorithms, robotics, team-based collaboration tools all wrapped up with smart computing and AI – allow us to redefine the way we work and network with anyone, anywhere, in real time. We can learn online and think for ourselves far more easily than ever before, allowing us to challenge the norm and reset the status quo. Most importantly, digital technology gives organisations the opportunity to bring ideas together; senior leadership can drive the business, right down to the operational coalface and vice versa. If we embrace digital technology, we can develop a positive, progressive digital workforce for the organisations of today and into the future.

While I was writing this edition of *The Digital Workforce* we experienced a global pandemic that mandated the transition to digital technologies literally overnight. The workforce started working from home where possible, supported by available technology. No longer were meetings held physically face-to-face; videoconferencing became the norm. Where people were still required to physically remain on a worksite, digital technology was used to communicate when staff were required, who was onsite, when staff members took a break and who they worked with, in case contact tracing was required.

We are also now confronted by a significant shift in the skills required to support the workforce of the future. According to the World Economic Forum, by 2025 there may be up to 85 million jobs displaced with 97 million new jobs required, resulting from a shift in the division of labour between humans and machines.[1] The top three new jobs are expected to focus on data science, AI and machine learning. We are also starting to see a shift in the types of employees that are most valued: employers are looking to attract people with passions that can be nurtured for the greater good, and the ability to adjust quickly and apply their previous experiences to new challenges without the need for prior learning. We will explore this further in chapter 3.

Everything we do now has a digital flavour: the way we work and the workforce itself transacts in digital. Digital is ubiquitous. It is the foundation of the digital workforce – the convergence of people, algorithms and machines – hence the title of this book. Today's organisations need to ensure that they are aligned to fully embrace the digital future.

I was inspired to write this book to achieve four goals:

1. To examine WFM through a business-focused lens, using real-life examples and expert opinions

2. To provide leaders and organisations with the intelligence required to predict and conquer key workforce-related issues

3. To help organisations maximise the value of their people, and ultimately overall organisation value, by building awareness of and leveraging the triggers that create people value

4. To present my proven 5-step workforce method, which can help any organisation deliver effective workforce management and value.

In the first edition of the book I had three goals. Goal number 3 – maximising the value of people – is new for this edition. If you can

---

1   World Economic Forum 2020, *The Future of Jobs Report 2020*, weforum.org/reports/the-future-of-jobs-report-2020.

'I have observed many vendor-led implementation methodologies that concentrate on successful implementation of the technology layer, but don't enable the changes necessary to deploy and adopt a digital operating model successfully.'

Jarrod McGrath

truly maximise the value of your people, the result will be happier, healthier employees and a brighter, more prosperous future for your organisation.

Further reading

The ROI of people

In Australia alone we're spending nearly a trillion dollars per year on people, and we have no idea of the ROI. In this new world of remote working, determining the ROI of your people is more important than ever.

Read the article at: smartwfm.com/book

McGrath, J 2020, 'Opinion: we're spending nearly a trillion dollars on people with no idea of ROI', The Mandarin, 12 November.

Very little has been written about what WFM is and, more importantly, how businesses can leverage its value. This book does both, but its main purpose is to teach you how WFM can benefit your business now and in the long term. Now more than ever, *The Digital Workforce* is compulsory reading for any leader or employee who wants to remain relevant in a modern world. It will give you the power to leverage technology and reimagine processes to place people at the epicentre of organisational success.

ABOUT THIS BOOK

The Digital Workforce is a how-to book for senior managers, project sponsors and project teams tasked with transforming their workforce in a disruptive, digital era. There are plenty of anecdotes, real-life experiences and examples to help explain the concepts that I introduce. In opening chapters I answer three key questions:

1. What is WFM and how did it evolve?
2. What are the benefits of WFM for your people and stakeholders?

3. How might digital change and artificial intelligence (AI) impact your workforce?

In chapters 4 to 9, I present the 5-step workforce method and show you how to use it to get WFM right in your business.

Having overseen many WFM implementation programs over the years, I have learned that the process to achieving success is predictable. So why do so few WFM programs meet their business objectives?

I discovered that there are differing views on how to extract value from the workforce. There is often a lack of pertinent, cohesive information to make an informed business decision and tie this back to the organisation's objectives. You only get the full picture when you speak to everyone who can influence or contribute to a business outcome: such as HR, finance, IT, operations and payroll.

I have developed the 5-step workforce method from my experience of numerous business transformation programs. I wrapped these experiences into a methodology that looks at success through your eyes, as well as the eyes of the business.

Here's what makes the 5-step workforce method different from other methodologies on the market:

- It's relevant to WFM *today*, and it includes the impact of digital and where the workforce of the future is moving.
- It can be used to support *any* phase of the WFM investment journey, from the beginning – alignment – to the final step – measurement – and everything in between.
- It's designed to be used in conjunction with vendor-led methodologies and industry-recognised project management methodologies, such as PMBOK and PRINCE2.[2]
- It's based on real-life experiences that represent a 360-degree view of the WFM market.

The final chapter, chapter 10, ties together the learnings from the previous chapters along with the trends identified in speaking to our

---

2   Perhaps the two most common methodologies to deliver IT projects.

experts to define the principals of maximising the value of people. We have all the people, processes and technology to support any organisation workforce evolution, inside the workplace and beyond.

> 'In the successful digital workforce, people – in partnership with algorithms and machines – are at the heart of every decision made. It's time to unlock the capability of the smart digitised team to ensure your organisation thrives today and into the future.'

Jarrod McGrath

HOW TO USE THIS BOOK

I encourage you to read *The Digital Workforce* from cover to cover, to ensure you gain the most value from your investment in this book. Alternatively, if you are looking for specifics, you can read relevant chapters and take out nuggets of information to help with your particular area of interest.

You will find some topics are covered more than once in this book, to reinforce and emphasise their importance, and to cater for readers who may 'dip in and dip out'.

Bonus: Smart WFM Academy and Microlearning Suite

To coincide with the release of this second edition of *The Digital Workforce* I am delighted to announce the Smart WFM Academy and Microlearning Suite. This is a great way to precede or review each chapter, test your understanding of key messages and principles and engage with other readers and myself. The microlearnings are mobile friendly and multimedia rich.

Find out more about the Smart WFM Academy and Microlearning Suite at: smartwfm.com/book

MEET THE EXPERTS

To help contextualise this book's learnings, I've included some fascinating insights from seven experts in digital WFM and human capital management (HCM).

Aron J. Ain, Chief Executive Officer, Chairman of the Board of Directors, UKG (Ultimate Kronos Group)[3]

UKG (Ultimate Kronos Group) CEO Aron Ain fiercely contends that there is a direct link between employee engagement, customer satisfaction, and business success. In April 2020, Kronos and Ultimate Software merged to become UKG, and Ain was tapped to be the CEO of the combined company with more than 13,000 employees and $3 billion in revenue. UKG is one of the largest cloud companies in the world as a leading global provider of HCM, payroll, HR service delivery, and workforce management solutions. Aron is the author of *WorkInspired: How to Build an Organization Where Everyone Loves to Work*.

Tracy Angwin – CEO at Australian Payroll Association

Tracy Angwin is a solutions expert, media commentator and popular keynote speaker, and the driving force behind Australian Payroll Association. Tracy is also the bestselling author of *The Payroll Revolution* and *Profit from Payroll*. She is sought out for commentary and guidance on all payroll topics including why employers get payroll wrong, optimising the payroll function and the future of payroll.

Jason Averbook – CEO and Co-Founder at Leapgen

Jason Averbook is a leading analyst, thought leader and consultant in the area of human resources, the future of work and the impact technology has on that future. He is the Co-Founder and CEO of Leapgen, a global consultancy helping organisations shape their future

---

3   In 2020, Kronos Incorporated and Ultimate Software merged to create UKG (Ultimate Kronos Group). Aron Ain is CEO of UKG.

workplace by adopting forward-looking workforce practices and fast-innovating technologies personalised for their business. Jason has more than 20 years' experience in the HR and technology industries and has collaborated with industry-leading companies in transforming their HR organisations into strategic partners.

Cian McLoughlin – CEO and Founder at Trinity Perspectives

Cian is the founder and CEO of Trinity Perspectives, a boutique sales training and consulting company specialising in win loss analysis and sales transformation.

Author of the Amazon number one bestseller *Rebirth of the Salesman*, Cian is a regular sales and marketing commentator in the mainstream media. Cian's blog has been voted one of the top 50 sales blogs in the world for the past four years. In 2020 he was selected as one of the top 50 sales keynote speakers in the world by *Top Sales World* magazine. In February 2021 Cian was voted as one of the top 100 sales voices on LinkedIn.

Cian is passionate about changing the perception of the sales industry and helping his clients to sell with integrity and authenticity.

Matthew Michalewicz – CEO at Complexica Pty Ltd

Matthew has more than 20 years' experience in starting and running high-growth tech companies, especially in the areas of AI, machine learning and decision optimisation. He is currently the CEO of Complexica, a provider of AI software for optimising sales, marketing and supply chain activities, and a director of several ASX-listed companies. He is also the author of five books, including the 2021 release *The Rise of Artificial Intelligence*.

Georgegina Poulos – Global Director People T2 and Global Retail Operations at Unilever

Georgegina is a senior executive with a strong human resources focus and extensive experience in both the international and domestic arenas across a variety of industries. Georgegina's expertise is in strategic human resources. She is a purpose-led leader – passionate about steering and implementing sustainable change, developing and empowering leaders and executing business strategy. As an organisational disruptor, she has a proven track record in assisting organisations to achieve sustainable business growth and a positive operating culture within complex multisite environments.

T2 is a chain of specialty tea stores with more than 80 stores globally, including in Australia, New Zealand, the UK, the US and Singapore. Sip by sip, it's building a generation of tea lovers on every continent – a brewing force for good coming together over the humble cuppa to celebrate our difference to make a difference.

Anna Santikos – Director of People, Culture and Learning at Montefiore

Anna is a human resources professional with over 17 years' experience spanning healthcare and construction. She graduated with a Bachelor of Economics before undertaking further postgraduate study at Sydney University, where she earned her Master of Labour Law and Relations.

With extensive knowledge of workforce planning, learning and development and talent management strategies, Anna joined Montefiore in 2009. She is responsible for human resources, staff wellbeing, and learning and development functions. Her current role also oversees the development and implementation of strategic workforce objectives, ensuring the achievement of organisational and service requirements. Anna is passionate about identifying and implementing initiatives and programs that place Montefiore as 'An Employer of Choice', support-ing a skilled and motivated workforce.

***

I've enjoyed the opportunities that have come from being involved in the people business both professionally and personally over the years, and I'm delighted and privileged to have been able to take the time out to write this book for you. I hope you find *The Digital Workforce* enjoyable and useful to drive people value into your business. Furthermore, I hope this book helps to broaden your horizons and make people-focused activities within the workplace more productive and enjoyable, improving the experience for all concerned.

It's time to challenge our traditional views about the way the workforce works. Don't accept the norm because it's 'the way it's done'. Be curious, think digital and get excited – you're about to kick off an ongoing transformational journey that will help you, your people, your organisation thrive both now and into the future.

All the best.

Jarrod

CHAPTER 1

THE EVOLUTION OF WORKFORCE MANAGEMENT

I have learned that very few people fully understand the benefits workforce management (WFM) can bring, how it fits into the overall HCM landscape, or the methods and learnings that can be successfully used to adopt it into their organisation. I was inspired to write this book to fill a gap in the marketplace. I'm passionate about encouraging leaders to learn from each other and reap the benefits digital transformation promises – for their organisations, their people and their customers.

When I first started working in WFM, I would have defined it as 'right person; right place; right time'. At the time, this definition would have been relatively accurate. In the early 2000s, I would have extended the definition to 'right person; right place; right time; right skills'. Today, WFM's role and benefits go far beyond this.

I recall facilitating a workshop at a prominent conference for HR and payroll professionals, where I posed the question, 'What is workforce management?' The responses I received were many and varied. They included:

- award interpretation
- payroll and costing
- work order management
- mobility
- employee self service (ESS) and manager self service (MSS)
- planning
- performance management.

The list of suggestions kept growing, but what stood out for me was that all the answers were different to mine. I also noticed that the definitions given were highly functional and transactional in nature – and all lacked a common understanding of what WFM is.

I've worked with many clients across a wide range of industries and unfortunately I've noticed a lack of understanding of WFM across the board. I've also realised that most stakeholders, senior leaders and employees don't care for any of these terms and acronyms – they just want to know whether the business is running efficiently, delivering on its brand promise and providing a great experience for employees and customers alike.

In the first edition of *The Digital Workforce* I created a one-line, in-a-nutshell definition of WFM:

WFM maximises people value, productivity and experience.

In this second edition I want to revise this definition to emphasise the importance of WFM to human capital management (HCM), HR and their associated digital strategies:

WFM is a foundational component of HCM, empowering the workforce from the coalface through to senior leadership to maximise people value and stakeholder return.

EXPERT INSIGHT

Aron Ain – CEO of UKG (Ultimate Kronos Group) – on the birth and evolution of workforce management

My career started with joining a small startup company called Kronos, which was in the business of automating that everyday business practice – the time clock – which hadn't changed since the 1950s. Who even imagined WFM would grow to be what it is? Or even that it would be called 'workforce management'?

In fact, I was involved with creating the term 'workforce management' back in 1982. We decided to coin the phrase because, when people thought about this technology-centric solution that was trying to automate the electro-mechanical world of mechanical time clocks, they immediately oriented themselves to think about it in simplistic terms – as opposed to all the dynamics of what a workforce management system could do. Our attempt to change the way people were thinking about the opportunity was starting a discipline called workforce management.

The mechanical time clock had always been the front-end of the payroll processing function. While payroll had been automated, if you will, the processes of gross-to-net calculations and printing pay cheques were still done manually, with organisations using time clocks or timesheets.

We created a device that looked like a mechanical time clock, but it wasn't: it had a microprocessor in it. Instead of just telling us when people came and went, the microprocessor gave us the ability to program work rules into the device. It would add up the punches and registrations, and apply the work rules, the awards and the collective bargaining agreements, according to individual company processes.

Now, that was exciting, but the problem was that in US terms, those devices were expensive. They cost about $5000 a device. We had a $5000 solution to a $2000 problem.

One of many turning points was in 1981 when IBM released the PC. We were able to take all the intelligence of this expensive device and, if you will, dumb it down to just become a data collection device. Then we put all the intelligence in this micro-computer. That opened up the possibilities to really expand all components of the software that was in the system, so that we could then move past just collecting data on when people came and went so we could pay them accurately, but also do all the other things that now are key and integral parts of workforce management. So, not only keeping track of when people come and go, but what they do while they're there, scheduling when they should be there, and so on. This was an everyday business practice that managers were doing manually, and it all related to workforce management.

Then the world moved from PC to local area networks. It moved from local area networks to wide area networks. It moved from there to client servers. It moved from there to the cloud. It moved from the web in its early forms to the web of today, and now it's moved to mobile, and social and AI – all still trying to attack the same problem of how to effectively manage a workforce.

As workforce management expanded, it became much more a function of the frontline managers who were responsible for making sure the right person was in the right place at the right time, and that employees were engaged and focused. It expanded from a payroll-centric function to making sure people worked accurately to a much more operational focus.

These days, customers are looking for something that can save costs and make sure they're in compliance and help drive productivity and those types of things, but I think, more importantly, as each day goes by, there's a deeper focus on driving business outcomes, delivering better service and increasing employee engagement. Those are things that people never thought about before in relation to WFM.

Read the full transcripts of my interviews with Aron at: smartwfm.com/book

WFM IS BORN OF INDUSTRIAL REVOLUTION

To really understand what WFM is, we need to go back to the 18th century and look at its evolution. Below is a brief chronicle of how WFM developed in line with waves of industrial revolution over the past years; how its ability to problem-solve impacted various areas of organisations; and the spread of WFM from its relevance to specific industries, to benefiting all industries and professions.

1760s–1860s

It all started with the advent of industry and industrialisation. People moved from farmland towards cities where manufacturing was beginning to take place. With this came the need for skilled workers and the commencement of ongoing efficiency and productivity improvements. This period is known as the First Industrial Revolution.

1870s–1960s

Figure 1.1 The Bundy Clock

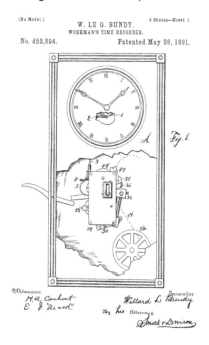

From the late 1800s a second phase of rapid standardisation, automation and industrialisation occurred, lasting into the early 20th century; this became known as the Second Industrial Revolution.

On 26 May 1891, Willard LeGrand Bundy patented the Bundy Clock – known as the 'Workman's Time Recorder' (see figure 1.1).[1] At a time when most labour was employed in mass production and on assembly lines, the clock was used to record workers' start and stop times. The Bundy Clock thus

---

1   Google Patents, Bundy Clock, google.com/patents/US452894.

increased the accuracy of hours worked and was, in effect, an early form of WFM.

Over time, these records were fed to payroll to increase the accuracy of workers' pay. So from the 1890s to 1960s, payroll and staff were the primary areas affected by the invention of the Bundy Clock, and manufacturing was the main industry to benefit.

1970s–2000s

The last three decades of the 20th century and the early 21st century brought the Third Industrial Revolution, which saw the invention of an 'online time clock' to coincide with the development of the microprocessor and the internet.

The first microprocessor-based time clock was developed in the late 1970s. It enabled the digital automation of time capture. Over time, these devices gradually improved to include self-service 'kiosk' functions, such as checking of leave balances, applying for leave and applying for an allowance.

Due to the online nature of these solutions, managers were able to see in real time who was at work; what shifts their team members were rostered to; whether their team members had the right skills; the cost of each person on any given shift; how much overtime had been incurred; and over-coverage and under-coverage of shifts. In some industries, such as health, retail, hospitality and contact centres, where staffing was impacted by demand, managers could see the impact of expected demand to forecast required staffing levels.

In this period of WFM evolution, some organisations elected to educate their supervisors to step up and become leaders and provided them with the required skills to develop their leadership ability. This delivered the tools to have a complete view of their workforce, including skills and skill gaps. These leaders could then work proactively with their team members and HR to focus on value-add areas such as staff development.

From the 1970s to 2000s, the impact of WFM had expanded from payroll and workers to include supervisors, information technology (IT), finance and HR. In addition, industries now affected by WFM had expanded to include those where WFM could add value, such as health, retail, hospitality and contact centres.

2010s onwards

The rapid development of digital technology – including mobility, tablets and wearables, and the development of artificial intelligence (AI), IoT, omni channel and machine-learning algorithms – coincided with our current period of advancement: the Fourth Industrial Revolution.

Likewise, WFM has evolved to provide intelligent solutions in real time, such as being able to analyse staff attendance data to send a predicted fatigue notification to a team member. WFM technology is able to trigger performance management events based on the number of employees who are late to work. Wearables provide hardware that can automatically register when a worker has arrived at work and when they have left work for the day. When a rostered worker is sick, WFM technology will automatically find a suitable replacement worker for their shift without any human intervention.

To help contextualise this, WFM and its impact across the broader HCM and payroll landscape might look something like figure 1.2 (on page 27).

Since the 2010s, WFM has expanded to include operations management, senior leadership and workforce robots. Workforce robots are robots that replace human roles that would need to be filled by a human if the robot was not there.

In summary, WFM now covers all industries, with digital wrapped around it to drive greater value.

So, what does this mean for you and your organisation?

Your organisation now has a much greater level of workforce information available. This information gives you a complete picture of your people, enabling you to improve workforce productivity, employee experience and overall people and organisational value.

'Technology innovation is occurring at such a rapid rate that it is difficult for organisations, policymakers and governments – let alone employees and customers – to keep up.'

▬

Jarrod McGrath

Figure 1.2: How WFM impacts business operations

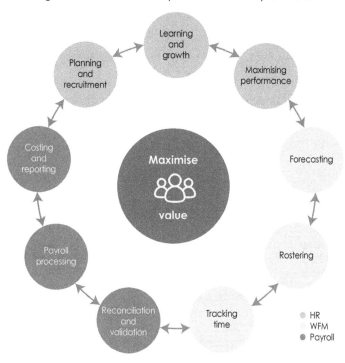

THE FOURTH INDUSTRIAL REVOLUTION AND WORKFORCE MANAGEMENT

Why do I draw a correlation between industrial revolution and the evolution of WFM? Throughout history, each industrial revolution has brought momentous change, and advances in WFM have been just as significant. As noted by Klaus Schwab,[2] two challenges face the Fourth Industrial Revolution, which might also limit the potential of WFM:

1. Changes in leadership might be necessary to facilitate large-scale transformation across economic, social and political systems.

2. There is a lack of narrative outlining the opportunities and challenges: if we are to empower a diverse set of individuals and communities, we need a strong narrative.

---

2   Schwab, K 2016, *The Fourth Industrial Revolution*, Penguin Books Ltd, London, UK.

In my view, WFM is no different. If business does not adapt to workforce change in a way that people can relate to and understand, the benefits of WFM will not be realised. This is clearly demonstrated in a Ventana survey, which found that only 7 per cent of organisations manage their workforce effectively.[3]

Figure 1.3 provides a summary of WFM's evolution, its impact on people and industries, and its correlation with the First, Second, Third and Fourth Industrial Revolutions.

Figure 1.3: The evolution of WFM

1760s – 1860s	1870s – 1960s	1970s – 2000s	2010s +
First Industrial Revolution	**Second Industrial Revolution**	**Third Industrial Revolution**	**Fourth Industrial Revolution**
Beginning of manufacturing, early efficiency and productivity movements	Mass production, electricity and assembly line	Semiconductors, mainframe and personal computing, internet	Ubiquitous computing mobility, AI, machine learning
Birth of industry	Start/stop accuracy, payroll	Scheduling, automated pay real time, kiosk	Forecasting, prediction flexibility, AI
Impact Staff	Impact Payroll, staff	Impact Payroll, staff ⊕ Supervisors, IT, finance, HR	Impact Payroll, staff, supervisors, IT, finance, HR ⊕ Operations management, senior management, workforce robots

---

3   Ventana Research, 'Workforce Management Value Index 2017, Vendor and Product Assessment', January, ventanaresearch.com/ value_index/human_capital_management/ workforce_management.

EXPERT INSIGHT

Jason Averbook – CEO and Co-Founder at Leapgen – on digital transformation

When I co-founded my business in 2017 I realised that organisations were not ready for what, at that time, we were calling the future of work. They were basically doing technology transitions, instead of true digital transformations. Organisations were moving from one technology to another, without really experiencing the gains that they should.

Right when Y2K ended, for those of us who remember that, we started talking about this thing called 'workforce 2020'. Workforce 2020 was going to be distributed and remote. It was going to be collaborative.

What did we really do between Y2K and 2020? Not a lot. And then, all of a sudden, we were hit with multiple pandemics: a new pandemic, which was a public health pandemic; and an old pandemic around diversity, inclusion and racism. Both pandemics accelerated our need as organisations to truly digitise.

And when I say digitise, I don't mean technology; I mean thinking differently. And when I say thinking differently, I mean answering questions like: how can I be agile in fragile times? How can I realise that roadmaps can't be three- to five-*year* roadmaps, but perhaps three- to five-*month* roadmaps? How can I put my employees at the centre of everything that I do, instead of putting my back office functions at the centre of everything that I do? And, most importantly, how do I plan for the fact that my business strategies might have to change on a dime?

None of us know what the future holds, but I will tell you that we've been talking about this for a long time. The pace of change will continue to increase, and I need to be ready as an organisation for that.

So, what does that mean? It means new operating models. It means new mindsets. It means new ways of thinking.

It means putting the employees at the centre, like I said, and it means making sure that I have agile technology that can shift and move as these macro moments pop up.

Read the full transcript of my interview with Jason at: smartwfm.com/book

Top take outs

- The term 'workforce management' was coined by Kronos in the early 1980s to expand people's thinking past recording the time employees started and finished their working day.

- The evolution of WFM has resulted in many more benefits being available to organisations today than in the past.

- We have moved from systems of record to systems of productivity to systems creating a unique workforce experience.

- It is important to understand the evolution of WFM is tied to industrial revolution, and that often significant change is required before companies can adopt its benefits.

- WFM cuts across most major functions in your organisation.

- My definition of WFM:

  WFM is a foundational component of HCM, empowering the workforce from the coalface through to senior leadership to maximise people value and stakeholder return.

Where to next?

I hope you enjoyed this informative background to WFM and its evolution. In the next chapter, we take a closer look at the benefits of digital WFM and the business problems it can solve.

CHAPTER 2

THE BENEFITS OF DIGITAL WORKFORCE MANAGEMENT

In business, it's tempting to look for some sort of technology solution to solve an intractable problem. In fact, every day software vendors the world over spruik the latest and greatest technology 'solution', desperately seeking customers to use it to solve their problem.

The drawback with this approach is that if a business constantly looks to technology to solve every issue, it overlooks a critical component of any successful business: its people. The key to solving most business problems (and I acknowledge this is a generalisation) is the need not just for processes, but people; not just logic, but emotion; not just technology, but humanity. This is where a holistic digital WFM strategy comes into play.

SOLVING BUSINESS PROBLEMS

So, what are the main WFM problems that businesses encounter, and what benefits can a company expect to accrue if it can solve them? Take a look at figure 2.1.

Figure 2.1: The far-reaching benefits of digital WFM

Each of these problems and solutions may be considered standalone, or there may be interdependencies with other areas. I have used a number of practical examples across a variety of industries to help explain this. While this list of the benefits you can achieve in your business is not exhaustive, you should be able to relate similar benefits to your workforce-related initiatives. You may also need to align the terminology to your specific industry.

Let's take a look at each of them.

Real-time visibility of people and costs

WFM allows for real-time capture and sharing of information.

From a capture perspective, WFM can determine who has arrived for work, what jobs they are working on and where the work should be costed.

From a sharing perspective, WFM allows staff to know where they are scheduled to work, what time they start and how long they will be required to work for.

> **Example:** Daniel is a nurse. He uses his mobile device to determine what time he starts work and what ward he will be working on today. Michelle, who is a nursing unit manager, knows that Daniel is at work and on the appropriate ward. Michelle is also able to track the actual cost of her team against the hospital department's budget.

Compliance

WFM is able to automate and build rules to manage compliance.

> **Example:** Allied Manufacturing Company creates an enterprise bargaining agreement (EBA), which sets out the payment rules and break rules for each worker type. The application of the rules can be automated, so the company knows that the payment and fatigue rules are being applied as expected.

Accuracy

WFM creates an environment that enables accurate recording and approval of time.

> **Example:** James works for a council and his job is to repair damaged roads. James works as part of a team and his team knows which roads they need to fix throughout the day in real time. James's manager can allocate his team to the associated tasks

required to fix the road. The costing information is then used by the council's operations team to understand the actual people cost associated with fixing the roads.

Full visibility of labour force

For you to effectively manage your people, you require complete visibility of the workforce. Consider each of your different worker types: full time, part time, casual, contract, seasonal and salaried.

Many organisations pay close attention to the mix of these worker types. There are factors that influence this form of analysis, including the payment conditions associated with the EBA and how they relate to the worker type.

Example: Murtuza changes the mix of full-time versus casual staff rostered to work on a specific shift. This change in staffing mix impacts the costs of the shift. Based on this, Murtuza is able to understand the impact of these costs in real time and make informed staffing decisions.

Forecasting

Once you have timely and accurate people costs, you can use this information to forecast.

Example: Melissa is the care manager in an organisation that provides health-based home care services. She can use the actual data to forecast her people costs for the next month.

Example: Herman is a store operations manager for a large retailer. He uses historical sales data to forecast the number of team members required to work in a certain department. This allows accurate people-cost forecasting.

Many other factors can also be used to forecast. In retail, this may include foot traffic throughout the day. In health services, it may include patient admissions data. In a contact centre, it may include expected call volumes due to an event.

Efficiency

WFM enables you to drive efficiency improvements.

Example: Before the implementation of a WFM system in a retail store, associate Mei received her task list of work to complete at the start of a shift from her manager, Jeanine. If there were changes to the task list during the day, Jeanine would need to find Mei and verbally communicate the changes to her. With the introduction of a WFM system, Jeanine can manage all her tasks for all her associates electronically. When the store gets busy, Jeanine can quickly reprioritise and communicate the tasks electronically, making the process more efficient.

Productivity

WFM enables you to drive productivity improvements.

Example: Before the implementation of a WFM system, the operators on a manufacturing line had many manual intervention steps to record start and stop times. With the introduction of WFM this process was automated. As a result, the production quantities increase along with productivity.

Culture and purpose

WFM allows your people to free up their time so they can concentrate on value-adding tasks to grow and drive company culture.

Example: Store operations manager Gary knows he has the right people with the right skills scheduled to work. This allows him to spend time with his people to understand their passions and for them to understand the organisational purpose, which was defined as part of the company's strategy as a key contributor in building company culture.

'The way we position and use technology to empower people and the business underpins effectiveness, competitiveness and an optimal operating environment.'

—

Jarrod McGrath

Employee experience and engagement

Many factors influence employee experience and engagement, and WFM is at the heart of this. WFM helps to make operational processes in your business more accurate, productive and efficient. Providing improved processes to people enables improved efficiency. These efficiency improvements allow time to be channelled away from administrative tasks towards value-adding tasks. Efficiency improvements make the workplace more enjoyable for your employees, which enables them to become more inspired about what they do, and this is reflected in their attitude towards your customers.

A *Harvard Business Review* report found that inspired employees are three times more productive than dissatisfied employees, yet only one in eight employees feels 'inspired'.[1] Knowing that your employees have less operational stress provides a platform to increase their engagement and make their work experience better.

> **Example:** Molly is a retail store manager. She used to complete her rostering using pen and paper. Now, due to the implementation of an automatic rostering system, Molly has an extra three hours per week to spend coaching her staff in areas such as improving product knowledge to enhance the customer experience.

EXPERT INSIGHT

Georgegina Poulos – Global Director People T2 and Global Retail Operations at Unilever – on employee experience

One of the biggest opportunities I see in regards to workforce management is in our ability to really understand and make the most of our people. In a traditional workplace you employ someone to perform a role, and they come to work to do that.

---

1 Garton, E 2017, 'What If Companies Managed People as Carefully as They Manage Money?', *Harvard Business Review*, 24 May, https://hbr.org/2017/05/what-if-companies-managed-people-as-carefully-as-they-manage-money.

Human capital systems can transform this experience by capturing people's career aspirations, hobbies, external learning and so on. It's about really getting to know our people beyond what we're specifically recruiting them for.

We need to have this data in a place where we can actually draw upon it, and give the team member the opportunity to opt in for different projects or use skills they might be learning at school in a different way. I think it's about real opportunity, really knowing our people, and seeing them beyond the role they're in.

Read the full transcripts of my interviews with Georgegina at: smartwfm.com/book

Further reading

Engaging staff isn't box ticking
Engaging your people and acting on their feedback is expected from the workforce, and critical to attract and retain great talent.

Read the full article at: smartwfm.com/book
McGrath, J 2019, 'Engaging employees is more than a one-time box-ticking exercise', *The Australian*, 22–23 June.

Customer experience

Likewise, many factors influence customer experience, and WFM provides a key ingredient: people personalisation of the experience. Customer experience is driven by a combination of many of the WFM benefits; in particular, culture, purpose and employee experience/ engagement. An inspired workforce can improve customer experience as your people believe in what they do and why they do it. This permutates to strong engagement with your customers and will result in a highly personalised customer experience. Personalised experience results in improved customer loyalty to your organisation's brand.

Example: Retail associate Sarah is able to understand her customers' needs, provide customers with options, communicate her company's purpose and provide an overall personalised experience that is meaningful to her customers.

EXPERT INSIGHT

Georgegina Poulos – Global Director People T2 and Global Retail Operations at Unilever – on customer experience

Entrepreneurial spirit is something that we harness at T2. We're a founder-led organisation; we like to take risks, we're a little on the quirky side, and we do that really well. We move really fast – changing gears is normal for us – but we really focus on the experience that the customer has, and that the team has. We need to shift the dial and continue to keep the customer first, and our team members and leaders need to savvy up in that commercial space, and give them the tools so they can be entrepreneurial. If they're not understanding their budget costs or their labour costs or their loss-prevention costs, then they can't really be entrepreneurial. Technology can really be helpful here. We can produce the data for the stores so they can actually run their business by being business owners, learning new skills; making sure that we've got the right people on at the right time to make sure the customer gets it, so it's all about the customer. It's not about cost-cutting, it's not about number-crunching, it's about giving our leaders access to data and helping them make decisions that benefit the customer.

Read the full transcripts of my interviews with Georgegina at: smartwfm.com/book

Increased sales/service output

If you are forecasting accurately and providing a superior customer experience, you are in a strong position to maximise your sales or service output. WFM allows you to track external factors and use this data to improve sales. For example, if you're in retail this may include data on previous buying trends, customer behaviour in the store, their likes from social media collated in real time and sent to the store assistant as part of the personalisation experience.

Example: Frank, an associate in a retail store, takes the time to fully understand his customers' needs. He spends time with each customer looking for opportunities to upsell, which results in increased sales revenue.

Example: James, a triage nurse in an emergency ward, takes the time to fully understand his patients' needs and ensures he accurately triages their condition at first point of contact. This results in allocation of patients to the most suitable doctor in the first instance, resulting in greater productivity and servicing a higher number of patients.

Quality

Quality manifests from a number of WFM and broader benefits.

Example: Nursing unit manager Michelle knows that her wards are adequately staffed from a people and cost perspective. Michelle is therefore able to focus on the quality of patient care provided.

Ensuring there are measures in place is important to track effectiveness. Your organisation can use this as a key point of difference to create a quality-focused mindset in your business and for your operational managers to take greater responsibility.

Leadership

WFM enables your organisation to develop leadership capability among your managers. Once you embed this entrepreneurial thinking, your leaders can take greater responsibility for commercial and people-related decisions. This will positively impact financial performance and lead to direct benefits for employee and customer experience. Having visibility of rosters in advance, and the cost of these rosters, allows proactive decisions on staff to be made prior to the event.

Example: Martin is a retail manager. He is able to make informed decisions about approval of overtime today. At the time of making his decision, Martin will be thinking, 'how will this impact our profit and loss? How will this impact my customers' experience? What skills development can I look to provide for my associates?'

Example: Dr Clarke runs an aged care facility. With the onset of COVID-19 she implements an automated rostering system to ensure contact tracing can be easily enacted. The system ensures that only team members who have completed mandatory COVID-19 training can be scheduled to work. It also helps Dr Clarke ensure that the minimum nursing hours per resident per day can be achieved while minimising the amount of overtime required. Dr Clarke also knows the cost of each shift in advance of the work being completed, so she can better mange organisational costs.

Further reading

COVID-19: the healthcare industry's long-overdue awakening
During the pandemic, healthcare professionals were battling to save lives every day. With frontline healthcare workers also falling ill to COVID-19, making staffing decisions became more difficult.

Read the full article at: smartwfm.com/book
McGrath, J 2020, 'Time to trace the workers', *The Australian*, 16 October.

WHAT WFM ROLES DO YOUR PEOPLE PLAY?

Solving intractable workforce-related problems requires people, process and technology skills. The list below (though not exhaustive) gives some sense of the multiple disciplinary skillsets required at every level of an organisation to drive the best possible WFM outcomes.

Looking through a business lens, this might cascade in the following way:

- Senior leadership identifies a business problem that may be fully or partially solved by the use of WFM. WFM could be used to reduce costs, increase revenue or maximise time spent with customers. This is often voiced to the rest of the organisation through a business strategy or an executive-sponsored project.

- Operations managers are tasked with addressing the problem and implementing a WFM solution. They need the skills and support to manage up and down in the organisation, and the ability to recruit and develop the right talent to deliver the outcome.

- Team members in the organisation need (a) the skills to support delivery of the solution to the problem; and (b) to be in a work environment that gives them scope to learn and grow.

- HR is the custodian of the overall people strategy, ensuring the right talent is available to meet current and future needs.

- Industrial relations (IR) supports the organisation when decisions are required that impact the employees and their industrial instruments. This role is often seen in organisations where unions are active.

- Payroll provides the services to ensure legislative compliance and financial integrity and ensures people are paid in a timely and reliable fashion.

- Finance provides the required financial metrics to report and measure the success or failure of areas of business or WFM initiatives.

- IT provides the systems and technologies to support WFM or other business solutions in a cost-effective and flexible way.

- Business specialists, either internal or external, are often required to bring all these components together harmoniously to create a working collective, focused on delivering a shared outcome.

EXPERT INSIGHT

Aron Ain – CEO of UKG (Ultimate Kronos Group) – on WFM benefits for employees and employers

When it comes to WFM, organisations are looking for a solution that can save costs and improve compliance and help drive productivity. But I think, more importantly, there's a deeper focus on driving business outcomes, delivering better service, driving employee engagement. Those are things that people never thought about before.

For example, if you're a retailer, and you can make sure you have the right person with the right skills in the right place at the right time, you will introduce a better customer experience; the customer will buy more from you, and that will impact your business outcomes.

If you're a hospital and you deliver better patient care by, again, in this example, having the right person in the right place with the right skills at the right time, then you will enhance your relationship with your customer – in this case, a patient, but still a client who has choices of where they go to get their healthcare provided.

If you're a manufacturer who's building a product and you can do it more effectively, more efficiently, and drive higher quality, your customer will benefit from that and you will drive better business outcomes.

Think about an employee who tells you what their optimal time to work is, and you can help them make sure they get there.

There's a community of people within your own organisation who can benefit from a modern workforce management solution. Look beyond just the obvious benefits to those areas where business outcomes can really be impacted by having a solution that will meet your needs, broadly defined. I think the days of just buying something that will automate the calculations or the award's interpretation are over and organisations are looking for more.

You need to make sure you understand that the employees of today and the managers of today expect access to information; they expect to be able to use devices and to interact, to communicate with the company about their own particular needs.

You need to understand this whole gig economy where everyone views themselves as being their own boss, even when they work at a workplace. Then you can provide solutions that broadly meet this new definition of work and you will be better equipped to recruit great people, retain great people, deliver great products, drive business outcomes.

Read the full transcripts of my interviews with Aron at: smartwfm.com/book

DELIVERING THE OUTCOMES

Once a business commits to delivering improvements via WFM, it embarks on a journey to deliver an outcome. A key aspect of large-scale change and delivering stated business objectives is adoption. Key performance indicators (KPIs) or goals are valuable to ensure the overall business benefit is achieved, ideally via changes to job roles, measures and incentives. Senior leadership should be continuously involved in the implementation, to ensure buy-in across multiple areas of the business. To implement KPIs or goals, the broader business areas and systems may need to be realigned to enable the changes and deliver the outcomes. This will help ensure the benefits flow to the operational manager and staff, who will in turn better understand the benefits being delivered.

To deliver people-related transformation is not easy and should not be underestimated. It requires senior leadership commitment and leadership to achieve these outcomes.

Top take outs

- The key to solving most business problems is for processes, people and technology to work together.
- There are many, varied business problems that digital WFM can solve.
- WFM cuts across numerous business functions and roles, which are all required to work collaboratively to deliver an outcome.
- To deliver true transformation requires senior leadership and operational commitment all the way to the coalface.
- KPIs or goals will enable you to streamline the way business benefits are achieved for your organisation.

Where to next?

This chapter has provided an understanding of the types of benefits you can achieve if you implement your WFM solution properly – and problems that can occur if not. The next chapter looks at the world of AI and what you might need to consider in its application.

CHAPTER 3

THE DIGITAL WORKFORCE AND ARTIFICIAL INTELLIGENCE

Much has been written in recent times about artificial intelligence (AI) and what it means for all of us. Is it a real possibility that machines will replace humans? A more realistic scenario is that humans will work together *with* machines – machines will help us solve specific business problems and improve productivity, freeing up our time for the head work of decision-making and heart work of relationship-building.

As we discussed in the preface of this book, the World Economic Forum predicts that by 2025, 85 million jobs may be displaced and 97 million new jobs created by the shift in the division of labour between humans, machines and algorithms.

This chapter further examines AI and the part it is playing in the digital workforce. In particular, we'll explore how AI is changing the way we work, and its impact on people.

WHAT IS ARTIFICIAL INTELLIGENCE?

You will find many definitions of AI but, in the context of WFM, AI is a collective term that incorporates the areas of automation, machine learning and deep learning to automate logical tasks that generally require human intelligence to solve a problem in areas requiring vision, hearing or speech.

Let's look at a simple application of AI in the workforce: the process of requesting a shift swap. The manual version of this process may look like figure 3.1.

Applying AI to this process removes the human intervention by the manager. The revised, automated process is captured in figure 3.2.

In the AI process, there is only one human interaction at the outset of the shift swap, and there are numerous benefits:

- AI removes the need for human back-and-forth to check and confirm the change.
- This frees up the manager's and employee's time for value-adding activities.
- The process ensures compliance and audit.
- It cuts down the time the process takes.
- It automates contact tracing (if required).
- There is a digital trail and data science can be applied to identify efficiency improvements into the future.
- AI tools start recognising individual behavioural patterns which helps with predictive analytics.

This also demonstrates the way AI technology becomes 'part of the team' – it does a real job and allows for better strategic workforce planning. In effect, AI becomes a bottom-line contributor to performance and cost.

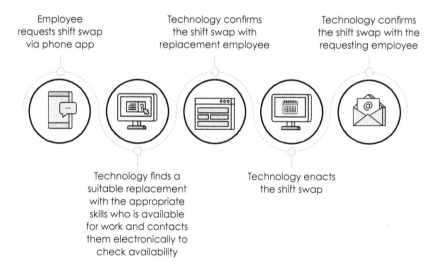

Figure 3.1: Manual process to request a shift swap

Employee contacts manager to change shift

Replacement employee confirms availability for work

Employee who requested the swap is notified of approval

Manager checks for a suitable replacement with the same skills

Shift swap is enacted

Figure 3.2: Process to request a shift swap using AI

Employee requests shift swap via phone app

Technology confirms the shift swap with replacement employee

Technology confirms the shift swap with the requesting employee

Technology finds a suitable replacement with the appropriate skills who is available for work and contacts them electronically to check availability

Technology enacts the shift swap

Workforce robots

I've mentioned already that we will see the introduction of what I call 'workforce robots'. These workforce robots will automate jobs that are currently undertaken by a human. For example, a workforce robot may take the frontline call in a contact centre and engage in a conversation with the caller to determine where to intelligently route the call.

'In the future work environment, humans will coexist with machines and algorithms; we will learn, develop and evolve together under a common framework. Machine and algorithm performance will need to be continually reviewed alongside human performance to ensure anticipated benefits are achieved.'

—

Jarrod McGrath

These workforce robots introduce a human dynamic to the workforce. If they break down, analogous to a person being sick, there will need to be a suitable workforce robot replacement. Alternatively, if there is no workforce robot replacement, a human replacement will need to be found to avoid interruption to the process. The major implication is that customers will no longer be able to interact with an organisation if there is no 'worker' (robot or human) there.

Workforce robots will need to be scheduled to complete a task, just like a human. This will be necessary so the business knows that the role associated with the frontline call is being fulfilled, even if it's by a workforce robot.

You might think workforce robots are akin to the robots that replaced workers on production lines years ago. But there's a key difference. Those robots *replaced* humans on the production line – the jobs were automated, never to be completed by humans again. The roles became part of the physical machinery used for production planning. Workforce robots, however, remain part of the human-based, planned workforce. They are interchangeable with human workers, rather than a replacement for them.

Automation

Another feature of AI is automation, which takes tasks that are completed by people and automates them. For example, consider data entry associated with time entries; manipulation of data; communicating digitally with other systems and so on. These are processes that can be taught by a human using software and executed by a machine. Automation can deliver many benefits, including:

- increasing quality of work, as it eliminates human errors
- improving productivity, as the process is always 'on'
- reducing costs by removing many human components of the task(s).

Georgegina Poulos – Global Director People T2 and Global Retail Operations at Unilever – on automation

I think automation is awesome. So many of us get stuck doing things that waste time. For me, automation isn't going to replace my role – it's actually going to free up time for me to focus on the things that are more important. It will allow me to be more strategic, more innovative and deliver better service.

Let's take the customer care space. There are some really basic questions that customers ask all the time: 'Where's my tracking information? When's my delivery due?' A lot of human hours are required for somebody to sit there and type responses out individually. Could they actually be doing other more important and enjoyable things, rather than that admin work? Absolutely.

I don't necessarily think the workforce is going to be halved due to automation. It's about re-skilling people and getting them to focus on other areas of work that are much more meaningful.

Read the full transcripts of my interviews with Georgegina at: smartwfm.com/book

Machine and deep learning

Machine learning builds on the concepts already in place for AI. It uses mathematical and statistical methods to find hidden insights and make predictions. For example, if an employee is continually late for work every Monday, machine learning could trigger a performance management record for that employee's manager to speak to the employee to take remedial action.

Deep learning builds on AI and machine learning to *continually* learn, just as the human brain does.

For example, an employee might habitually request to work each Wednesday afternoon. Using machine-learning techniques, the system will be able to predict this request and make the process more efficient by automating this request each week.

Over time, deep-learning techniques may identify that while working on Wednesdays, the employee is 20 per cent more productive, and the deep-learning algorithm determines that on Wednesday the employee completes their allocated work in a shorter shift, resulting in the same quality output. This learning is then applied to optimise shift lengths for all employees, resulting in decreased shift length, lower labour costs and the same quality output.

The benefits of machine learning and deep learning are far-reaching. For example, workforce robots will learn from human interactions, performance improvement and develop their knowledge base, and predictive learning will offer cause, effect and solution options to people.

EXPERT INSIGHT

Matthew Michalewicz – CEO at Complexica Pty Ltd – on our changing understanding of AI

The biggest shift I've seen during my career is our changing perception and understanding of AI. Back in the '80s, my father – an AI professor – gave presentations to business people as part of his university work. In one lecture, one of the executives raised their hand and said, 'Excuse me, Professor. I just wanted to interrupt and ask a question. Is AI ... like what is that? Are we talking about aliens here?' As funny as that sounds today, general understanding was so limited back then, even though there was a lot of research being done in the field; whereas today, automation of jobs has become a mainstream topic. That said, most people still don't understand exactly what it is, but at least they have heard of it.

Behind the scenes, you've got a progression around the technology, especially in the area of machine learning: deep-learning algorithms that are coupled with computing power and the internet, which provides sources of digital data boosting text and its image to train machines on. All of that has allowed the progress technologically of AI. But progress is not as fast or significant as the market awareness and hype that's been created around it.

So, what exactly is AI? Well, I think you can break it into two categories. The first is general AI, which is the recreation of the human mind in a digital form that allows for emotional interpretation, decision-making, creativity. This is what most people imagine when they think of AI. In my view we are a long, long way away from that becoming a reality.

Then there's this other area of AI – let's call it specific AI – which is problem-specific. It's the application of technology to specific problems. The problem could be detecting fraud in credit card transactions; it might be detecting patterns and images; it might be used in security.

I think that's where a lot of misunderstanding or confusion arises. People see AI in the movies, they see the hype, and they think of general AI; whereas the major advances today are really around the specific applications.

I also think some of the hysteria and misunderstanding around AI is due to people suddenly discovering it because it has been featured in the media, and because they've never heard of it before they assume the field is growing really quickly. They've suddenly come across it, but it's been happening since the late '40s. It's old and incremental in development. If people had been following the industry for the last 70 years, they wouldn't think much of it. They would see incremental advancements that are being made, but they wouldn't have the view that there are big, scary changes right around the corner, which I don't think there are.

I've noticed people connecting innovation and AI and making a direct link to the workforce. They're saying AI and innovation is bad because it's going to eliminate jobs and so forth. But this is missing the most important part of that equation: capitalism. It's not AI that's driving these disruptive changes, it's not even innovation, it's none of those things – it's capitalism. We're in a free market capitalistic society, which means that if I'm hired as CEO or I'm on the board of directors of a company, then my legal duty is to value shareholders. My job is to maximise the value of that company, protect it from risk, make good decisions and so on. Basically, we're operating in an environment where every company is being driven by people who are trying to maximise the value of those companies for the shareholders. That's how dividends are paid, that's how the business world works.

However, the problem is that the people who are trying to fulfil their managerial directorship duties and maximise shareholder value view reducing labour as one of the most obvious targets for increasing shareholder value. So, my business outcome is that I want to cut my labour by 10 per cent. How do I do that?

Then you think, here's an interesting technology, AI, and maybe it could help me eliminate people. You make this connection – AI eliminating jobs – but AI is not what's driving the elimination of jobs. It's capitalism.

Because if I eliminate the jobs, I make more profit as a company, and that increases shareholder value. The company becomes more valuable. If I'm an executive, I'm likely to make my bonuses then.

Entrepreneurs are sitting to the side and saying, 'Hey, these big companies want business outcomes like cutting labour, so I'm going to create an AI company that will help them eliminate the labour, help them achieve their business outcomes, and if I do a good job by building a good piece of software and delivering on my promise, I'll become a billionaire in the process.' That's a capitalism driver as well.

I think what is really driving all the change in the world today is not the goodwill of humanity or corporate social responsibility, it's none of those things … What's driving all of this today is capitalism. It is how our society is set up. That is, in my view, one of the most interesting things to explore.

Think about it like this: if a business's goal is to protect jobs over time, that business will become uncompetitive and most likely will fail, costing all of those jobs. For example, look at the automotive industry in the US: it collapsed, and all of those companies went into bankruptcy. They had huge unions protecting all of the jobs. They resisted technology. They became uncompetitive and went into bankruptcy, firing all those people the unions had tried to save.

Most AI systems that we deploy are not designed to replace people – they're to help people make better decisions and become more effective in their jobs. Think about retail liquor stores: decisions about which products should go on sale at a particular time are based on AI intelligence which is then used by human experts in these businesses to augment their own experience and knowledge. Because of AI technology, real workers are able to make better decisions, be more competitive in the marketplace and thereby actually retain their jobs.

When a technology comes along that can make a process more efficient, there's usually a job loss. However, there is an equal creation of jobs for companies that need people and skills to enable that technology, build products, deliver services around businesses, and so on.

I look at AI as just one of many, many technologies available to companies to improve their performance, and that's what a CEO is hired for. It's not to maintain or to decrease performance, it's to improve it. And if AI can increase the performance of a company, then the people who are in that company and all of those jobs become more secure than they otherwise would have.

The ultimate scary scenario people fear is the merging of technology with the brain. There has been an enormous number of studies predominantly on animals involving cutting out pieces of the brain, then embedding processing chips into the brain to make up for the pieces that have been cut out. Imagine 20 years from now being able to get a chip in your brain that gives you a photographic memory, which would enable you to have the entire *Encyclopedia Britannica* accessible in your mind. Eventually, the chip could be connected to the internet.

We could see things like electronic telepathy, where you can just think and form messages and send them to other people. This is probably the area that is, for me, the most frightening and the most realistic because it could happen. Once you augment the human body, everyone wants that kind of augmentation because it becomes a competitive disadvantage not to be augmented.

I don't think it will bring on the Fifth Industrial Revolution, but that's one of the subjects that's worth looking at over the next 20 years and seeing it how it unfolds.

Read the full transcripts of my interviews with Matthew at: smartwfm.com/book

THE DIGITAL WORKFORCE – CHANGING THE WAY WE WORK

I like to think of the digital workforce as the convergence of machines, algorithms and people – hands, heads and hearts (see figure 3.3).[1]

Figure 3.3: The digital workforce

Machines	⊕	Algorithms	⊕	People
Hands		*Heads*		*Hearts*

The incorporation of machines and algorithms into our daily work lives is only going to become more prominent. Figure 3.4 depicts the World Economic Forum's expectation of the changing division of labour between humans and machines.

---

1   Boston Consulting Group, Jason Averbook and others have also described the digital workforce using the hands, head and heart metaphor.

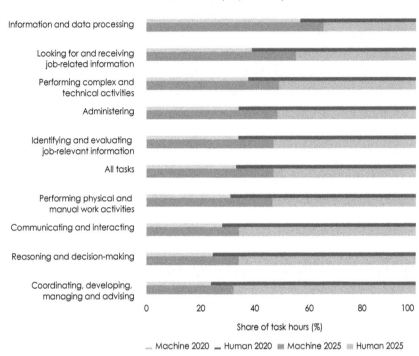

Figure 3.4: Share of tasks performed by humans versus machines, 2020 and 2025 (expected)

Source: World Economic Forum 2020, '*The Future of Jobs Report*'

As you can see, it is the repetitive tasks such as information and data processing that are expected to be automated, allowing humans to focus on tasks such as coordinating, reasoning, developing, managing and advising.

I'm hoping that by now you are starting to understand the potential that digital WFM, supported by advances in AI, has to change the way we work. The changes will continue in greater numbers and at a faster rate as they are embraced in our workplaces and we start to value the benefits that they bring.

Now, let's look in more detail at some of these changes to the way we work, and the skills required to manage this.

Note: since writing the first edition of *The Digital Workforce*, COVID-19 has significantly impacted the world and the workforce.

The following topics were all covered in the first edition, but every single one has accelerated at warp speed or simply become adopted as common practice more quickly than we could have predicted.

Networks

The world is now essentially one large, interconnected network that will continue to grow. People are connected, machines are connected, information is connected. We have moved from a world of person-to-person connection, to node-to-node connection.

These changes bring many benefits: we have access to a world of knowledge; we can use this knowledge to learn; we can mobilise quickly; we can flex up and down quickly; we can see things in real time, and so on.

This means the way we work has become highly responsive, focused, agile and available 24/7.

Remote work

The network concept also enables us to mobilise highly specialised people and teams with specific skills across the globe, in real time. At Smart WFM we have witnessed a sharp increase in clients and their employees working remotely, and this extends across international boundaries.

Remote work has become the normal way of operating. Collaboration technology has reached a tipping point where we can virtually interact as if another person is in the room with us. Augmented reality and virtual reality will also enhance this experience over time. For example, the consultant will be able to see your building in 3D through a headset and communicate with you as if they were there on the premises – say a store or a hospital.

Just as we are now able to source appropriately skilled people from across the globe, the concept also applies to teams. Highly skilled teams with the knowhow to solve specific business problems will work remotely (or, perhaps, onsite) to complete a defined project or achieve a particular outcome.

For example, my team at Smart WFM was recently engaged by a global quick service restaurant (QSR) group that was looking for practical advice on the best way to structure its supply chain and store operations across its many hundreds of US-based sites. We quickly formed a team with our sharpest minds, engaged with the customer to understand its business goals and worked with it to deliver the desired outcomes. Our team was spread across multiple Australian and US cities, which was totally acceptable to the customer – it knew the team with the right skills to deliver their outcomes was on the job.

EXPERT INSIGHT

Georgegina Poulos – Global Director People T2 and Global Retail Operations at Unilever – on people experience

Globally, our workforce are Millennials. We have an extremely young workforce. They've grown up with an iPhone, a laptop, a tablet. Our team members are tech-savvy. We need to be able to adapt our processes and our mediums to support this new workforce. This new workforce expects things to be digital, expects things to be available on any device, anytime, anywhere.

We can't live in a world where we're expecting people to do manual leave forms or manual change-of-status or sending in résumés. A, it's not efficient for us. B, we're not capturing data. C, it's not right for the environment because it uses too much paper. Our consumer doesn't live that way, our team member doesn't live that way. We have to use digital technology, and it has to be mobile.

That's why our new system's accessibility is a real winner: it's available on any device at any time, anywhere, so it's easy for team members to log on and for leaders to manage.

Read the full transcripts of my interviews with Georgegina at: smartwfm.com/book

Reskilling

The World Economic Forum expects there to be an overall increase in the number of jobs during the coming five years – despite many existing jobs becoming obsolete. Aron Ain – CEO of UKG (Ultimate Kronos Group) – lists Amazon, FedEx and DHL as examples of companies that are increasing staff numbers despite the increased use of automation.

EXPERT INSIGHT

Aron Ain – CEO of UKG (Ultimate Kronos Group) – on the division of labour between humans and machines

I don't think automation is going to replace our need for human workers. Customers expect more service and more innovation nowadays, and it takes humans to deliver those things.

People are more valuable than ever. Just look at Amazon: arguably the most automated company in the world in terms of how it delivers its business and services. It's up to more than 1.13 million employees now – it hired 248,500 additional employees during quarter three, 2020 alone. We're not going to automate ourselves away from people; it's just not going to happen.

Logistics companies FedEx and DHL can't keep up with demand, either; they can't hire people fast enough. These are distribution companies that are highly automated, but they still can't get away from hiring people.

Technology is here to stay, and I think we need to embrace it and think about how we can use it in various forms to enhance the experiences of our customers, the lives of our employees and the future of our businesses.

Read the full transcripts of my interviews with Aron at: smartwfm.com/book

With this increase in jobs, however, we have a conundrum. The new division in labour will result in some roles being made redundant while new roles requiring different skills are created. Eventually, economies will need to find jobs for the people who are not working today.

Check out figure 3.5 to see how the World Economic Forum sees this taking place.

Not surprisingly, the key roles with increasing demand into the future are focused around data analytics, AI, machine learning and process automation; while roles with decreasing demand are those that are repetitive in nature, such as data entry, administration, book-keeping and payroll clerking.

The same report also noted that employers expected that reskilling for these new roles would take six months or less.

Figure 3.5: Top job roles increasing and decreasing in demand

Increasing demand	Decreasing demand
1 Data analysts and scientists	1 Data entry clerks
2 AI and machine learning specialists	2 Administrative and executive secretaries
3 Big data specialists	3 Accounting, bookkeeping and payroll clerks
4 Digital marketing and strategy specialists	4 Accountants and auditors
5 Process automation specialists	5 Assembly and factory workers
6 Business development professionals	6 Business services and administration managers
7 Digital transformation specialists	7 Client information and customer service workers
8 Information security analysts	8 General and operations managers
9 Software and applications developers	9 Mechanics and machinery repairers
10 Internet of Things specialists	10 Material-recording and stock-keeping clerks
11 Project managers	11 Financial analysts
12 Business services and administration managers	12 Postal service clerks
13 Database and network professionals	13 Sales rep, wholesale/manuf tech and sci products
14 Robotics engineers	14 Relationship managers
15 Strategic advisors	15 Bank tellers and related clerks
16 Management and organisation analysts	16 Door-to-door sales, news and street vendors
17 FinTech engineers	17 Electronics and telecoms installers and repairers
18 Mechanics and machinery repairers	18 Human resource specialists
19 Organisational development specialists	19 Training and development specialists
20 Risk management specialists	20 Construction labourers

Source: World Economic Forum 2020, *The Future of Jobs Report.*

Matthew Michalewicz – CEO at Complexica Pty Ltd – on universities in the digital normal

AI came out of universities. I spent my childhood in a university. My father was a professor of AI from when I was six years old. As a child, I would go to my father's office and play video games while he talked about neural networks or machine learning techniques with PhD students. I came from that environment, and AI came from that environment. Like a lot of technologies, AI has become much more widespread, much more commercialised; however, its roots still go back to that education setting.

It's essential that universities are part of the conversation because that's where the scientists are working on algorithmic advancement. The thing that has changed over the last 20 to 30 years is that a lot of companies – such as Apple, Facebook, Amazon and Microsoft – have created massive research centres of their own. Smaller organisations like Complexica, which are too small to have their own scientific research team, partner with universities and collaborate with them on research.

Read the full transcripts of my interviews with Matthew at: smartwfm.com/book

Education mindset

With reskilling top of mind, the way in which we educate people becomes more important than ever. Moving forward, I see an entire shift in education. Traditionally, most of our theoretical skills were learned at university or centres of advanced education. Often, real-world skills were learned after university when we commenced work.

Today's generation is now googling its way through life, using lateral and logical ways to solve problems in an instant. If we work backwards, we now need to commence technology and business education

'There is a significant responsibility on the employer to ensure that they have the appropriate people-support networks and learning paths in place to future proof their people. I am a believer of balancing school, formal education and on-the-job training aligned with people's passions to maximise people and organisational value.'

Jarrod McGrath

at a very early age. Traditional curriculums will still have relevance, but new subjects and skills will need to be added in an agile manner.

Education will become highly focused on the specific task at hand, with subjects becoming personalised to the needs of each student. The World Economic Forum reports that 94 per cent of employers expect employees to pick up new skills on the job.[2]

At Smart WFM we invested heavily to build a graduate and mentor program to support our workforce.

Over the coming years, mentoring and skills development will be a high-focus area; I believe it will become a key influence area when it comes to attracting and retaining talent.

EXPERT INSIGHT

Jason Averbook – CEO and Co-Founder at Leapgen – on education in a digitally transformed world

I think it's really important that we stop educating people on a just-in-case basis, and focus on a just-in-time basis. What does that mean? It means we no longer send young people to university for four to six years, where they'll learn all this stuff just to get a degree and hope something they're taught will be useful in the future. The current way of working just moves too fast for that.

What's more important is that people have a baseline on which they can learn and unlearn. As organisations, we have to give our workers a real-time education on the job, as technologies and new ways of working invent themselves.

As change continues to happen, we need to provide our workforce with opportunities to get up to speed on that change. That doesn't mean giving them training on Microsoft Excel or Word; your people can learn a lot of that stuff on their own. (Notice how, in 2020, when we were all forced to learn

---

2   World Economic Forum 2020, *The Future of Jobs Report 2020*, weforum.org/reports/the-future-of-jobs-report-2020.

how to use Zoom, Teams and Slack, people just magically figured it out? I can tell you that in January 2020, organisations that we were working with would say there's no way their workforce is ready for Teams or to work remotely. Being forced into it changed everything.)

Over the past five to seven years, our thinking around education has changed. Before that, people used to say that if you have an MBA, you're guaranteed a job. People don't even look at your résumé to see you have an MBA anymore. You'd be hired for your background in AI before an MBA. That's because, as an employer, I know I can mould your knowledge about AI to what the organisation needs more easily than I can mould your MBA.

I truly believe that the education system needs to transform in light of this. Universities, in order to stay relevant, have to adjust to the way that the world of work is hiring and growing workers.

Read the full transcript of my interview with Jason at: smartwfm.com/book

Ability

There is a growing focus on innate ability and learning capability within the workplace. We have reached a point where companies are hesitant to throw money at learning that becomes obsolete in a very short timeframe. Companies will need to think about ability or capability paths which, with the help of AI, can determine the best way to leverage current knowledge.

The other important factor to consider is the change in emphasis from 'employer knows best' to 'employee passion', and how organisations embrace employee passions within their work environments. If we can align employee passion with organisation direction (rather than creating rigid business plans for employees to follow), learning takes on a completely new direction. We will shift from thinking statically about future roles to leveraging individual passions to grow into future

'The experience of COVID-19 showed us that we don't need nearly as much time to realign as we previously thought.'

—

Jarrod McGrath

roles. It's a big mindset change and it feels rather unnatural, because we tend to have fixed views on what business planning is.

A number of organisations were fast enough to reposition people into new roles rather than making them redundant. COVID-19 helped us to recognise our outdated views on human capability.

Will we see a lower uptake of university degrees, as young people realise they can acquire a sufficient knowledge set to bypass this stage of pedagogy? I think so.

Top take outs

- The digital workforce is the convergence of machines, algorithms and people – hands, heads and hearts.

- Remote work, team-based work and self-management are the new normal.

- Some jobs will be replaced by workforce robots, but a human will still be required to complete them if the workforce robot is out of action.

- In the future work environment, humans will coexist with machines and algorithms; we will learn, develop and evolve together under a common framework.

- Organisations will need to address the impact on workers; some roles might disappear, while other roles might change considerably and require reskilling.

- Organisations will shift from thinking statically about future roles to leveraging individual passions to grow into future roles.

- AI can be considered in two categories: *general* AI where the human is fully recreated by a machine, and *specific* AI where specific problems are solved by machines.

Where to next?

I hope this chapter provided you with an understanding of how technology and AI is playing out in the world of WFM.

In the next chapter I'll introduce the 5-step workforce method and lay out the fundamentals you need to ensure the success of WFM initiatives in your organisation.

CHAPTER 4

INTRODUCING THE 5-STEP WORKFORCE METHOD

Having had the privilege of working with many organisations on their WFM initiatives, I've realised the WFM investment process is highly predictable; the same problems occur, over and over. So, I've identified a number of key areas of the WFM investment process that, if enacted correctly, will ensure that the investments you make in WFM return the defined business benefits you are seeking. Following this methodology will help develop your workforce, tighten its culture, improve brand loyalty and strengthen alignment to organisational goals.

From my experience I have seen many organisations, in particular product suppliers, focus on implementation. While implementation is an important step in the process, it is only one step that your organisation needs to undertake. Hence, the methodology I have created – the 5-step workforce method – looks at the *entire* WFM lifecycle. You can adopt the method at any of the five steps, moving back and forth between each step relevant to your business initiative, as depicted by the bidirectional arrows in figure 4.1.

Top of mind in this methodology – however you enact it – is people.

By way of introduction to the 5-step workforce method, let's take a look at figure 4.1.

Figure 4.1: the 5-step workforce method

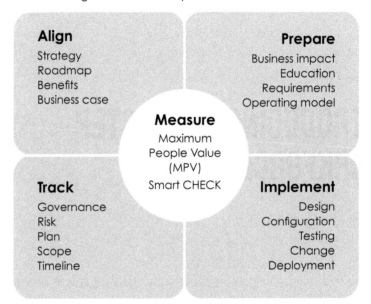

Each of key steps of this method is covered in detail in a separate chapter, but let's take an overview of them now:

- **Align:** Make sure you understand your business strategy; align it to your workforce goals and create a baseline to achieve your WFM outcome.

- **Prepare:** Ensure your business is educated and ready for the transformation journey ahead. This includes confirming alignment between senior leadership, operations, finance, HR, payroll and IT, and understanding the expected business impact.

- **Implement:** Implement your processes and technology; deploy your system and empower your people to adopt it effectively.

- **Track:** Confirm governance is in place to mitigate risk, ensure compliance and keep your WFM initiative moving along, balancing the inputs from your various business stakeholders.

- **Measure:** Continually review the benefits to ensure you receive optimal value from your WFM initiatives and maximise your people and organisational value.

Smart CHECK

Irrespective of where you are in your business lifecycle, awareness of your current position is highly beneficial, if not mandatory. A Smart CHECK will generally look at people, process and technology and guide your decision-making about your next steps.

The Smart WFM team can help you undertake a personalised Smart CHECK for your organisation.

Find out more at: **smartwfm.com/book**

TIPS FOR SMARTER IMPLEMENTATION

Before we drill down into the five steps, here are some tips to make sure you avoid mistakes I have seen made in the past that make WFM implementation more difficult.

Focus on storytelling with your team

In the past I have seen many WFM initiatives become overcomplicated and consumed by technical and IT speak, which has prevented stakeholders getting to the point quickly. When you speak about your WFM initiative, be conversational in your delivery, speak in plain English and avoid (or explain) jargon. Tell a story; this will ensure complete engagement with your audience.

Georgegina Poulos – Global Director People T2 and Global Retail Operations at Unilever – on storytelling

Your WFM project has to have a brand. It needs to have its own identity so you can really have some fun with it to gain traction.

We called ours 'Belong2'; because you belong, we belong. To do this well I think you need to understand your imperative for change. What is it that is really in it for your people? What are the factors that are getting you to change, and what does success look like? Leaders who are leading the change need to be storytellers, bringing the team along, because change is scary for anyone. If I know why I'm doing it, what's in it for me, what I'm going to get out of it, and what role I need to play, then I'm more likely to get on board.

Read the full transcripts of my interviews with Georgegina at: smartwfm.com/book

Remember, the 5-step workforce method is not a silver bullet

It's important to note that this method is not the answer for every business challenge you have; it isn't a silver bullet. Rather, it is a framework that can be applied to help guide you through your workforce-related business improvement. The method is designed to be used collaboratively with traditional methodologies and/or vendor methodologies – not to completely replace any methodology or process you already have in place in your organisation.

Understand your organisational goals

Your organisation's senior leadership will be looking to achieve business success in several ways: by increasing the addressable market, increasing revenue, retaining the best staff, decreasing costs and/or reducing risk. WFM can help deliver on these business objectives. It will help if you prioritise these objectives and align your organisational goals to your workforce goals. Each time you make a decision, reflect on your organisational goals.

EXPERT INSIGHT

Matthew Michalewicz – CEO at Complexica Pty Ltd – on the importance of starting with your organisational goals

My father, a professor of AI, taught me that you shouldn't look at digital transformation from the point of the technology – you should look at it from a business outcome perspective. In other words, the first question to ask has nothing to do with AI or even technology – it's around the business outcomes you want to achieve.

Everything begins with a vision or a goal or a set of problems that an organisation wants to address. And then you work backwards to work out which skills you need in the organisation to achieve that; what technology you need; what data you might be missing.

As an organisation, you're saying, 'This is what I've got; what do I need in the future?' It's impossible to answer that question without having a clear vision of what you want the organisation to look like. Then, you go backwards into the people, technology systems and processes that will support your future state.

Read the full transcripts of my interviews with Matthew at: smartwfm.com/book

Make sure your workforce is engaged

Senior leadership, HR, operations, payroll, IT and finance must all be aligned to the business objectives. In addition, programs of work across these business areas need to align resources and outcomes to avoid contention and misunderstanding. Special attention should be placed on HR and operations functions to make sure they are working together, as both are tightly coupled to business operations.

Define benefits and measures

In chapter 2 I introduced the far-reaching benefits WFM could have within your organisation. Take a look back at these, pictured in figure 2.1, now.

Benefits must be defined in an easy-to-understand way. For example, if the business goals are to decrease labour costs and increase productivity, ask:

- How will these goals be achieved?
- How will these goals be measured?

These benefits and measures must be tightly aligned to goals and, ultimately, business requirements. Chapter 9 introduces a benefits and measures framework.

EXPERT INSIGHT

Anna Santikos – Director of People, Culture and Learning at Montefiore – on alignment and planning

I've been with Montefiore, an aged care provider based in the Sydney area, for over 10 years. Montefiore has quite a long and extensive history, spanning over 130 years.

In the time that I've been in the sector we've experienced a number of challenges. Over the last few years, some of those challenges have intensified and of course we've also had new ones emerge.

The Royal Commission into Aged Care Quality and Safety has placed the industry under enormous scrutiny, particularly when we reflect on the media coverage. In saying that, though, it's also very well recognised that this is such a rare opportunity to review and hopefully reshape aged care services in Australia and ultimately improve quality care outcomes for our aged population.

There's also the issue of funding. Different surveys have shown that the overwhelming majority of providers believe that current financial pressures impact and limit their ability to be able to provide quality services – the services that our elderly deserve to receive. In line with our Mission and Vision as an organisation, we continue to seek to be able to deliver quality services and be able to build and improve on those services. At the same time, we must make sure that we're attracting the best-quality workforce that we possibly can to deliver those services. So there's a real tension there.

Our Leadership Team develops and reviews our strategic plan. We collaborate with different stakeholders to devise that plan. It is then endorsed by our Board and we continue to work through the different objectives that we identify through that plan.

One of the things that we have found really, really valuable is having a Workforce Steering Committee which meets fortnightly. We have different representatives that participate on that committee. Being able to collaborate around different initiatives and just make sure that we are staying on track in terms of our people initiatives and how they link in with our corporate strategic plan has been invaluable.

At Montefiore, being a not-for-profit, there is also a genuine commitment to reinvestment into services. We are constantly looking at ways we can improve, while ensuring that we operate within a financially viable framework. We're never complacent.

We try to use technology effectively across a number of different areas. We have a very strong focus on how we can utilise technology to improve our current workflows and processes, so we can achieve efficiencies and ultimately free up our people to be with our consumers. Having that engagement is just so important in terms of our people strategy, and in terms of being able to deliver great services to our consumers.

We've also relied on technology to support some of our communication requirements. Technology can very efficiently support us to cover off the quite extensive compliance and legislative requirements we need to adhere to and this is a current area of focus for us.

We're also focused on how we can optimise the experience for our staff working at Montefiore. An example of that would be the Learning Management System (LMS) we implemented a couple of years ago. I think it's fair to say that this has enabled us to build on the strong learning culture that we have at Montefiore. We have a commitment to supporting staff learning and the implementation of the LMS is an example of this.

Another example is the online recruitment and onboarding system we implemented last year, which was very successful. We've received really positive feedback from a number of new hires around the onboarding experience. It's left a very positive impression.

Now, we're really keen to finalise the deployment of our Workforce Management System (WFM) which is key to supporting our workforce management practices. This system will assist managers to look after their teams by utilising our people resources more efficiently. We see that as being key to our overall staff engagement workforce strategy.

One of our key learnings throughout our transformation process has been making sure that we spend the required time upfront scoping as an organisation, and identifying our requirements. It's all about considering what you need in terms of your processes – what they should look like, and how technology can help you work through those processes in a more efficient way.

Read the full transcript of my interview with Anna at: smartwfm.com/book

Understand the change, culture and mindset shift required to transform your organisation

In my experience, this is the biggest hurdle to overcome to achieve desired outcomes – and it is becoming even more important as we see a shift towards hybrid working, where at least some employees are working remotely. The greater the change, the more your people's involvement is required. As your workforce moves to a digital way of working, the underlying organisational core may need to change. Due to automation of processes, roles may change within the operations area of the organisation, such as: completing daily scheduling, taking responsibility for cost management, increasing staff interaction and goal-setting in line with organisational needs.

Don't bite off more than you can chew!

Focus on outcomes that align with your overall WFM maturity, the size of your organisation and specific localisations associated with your organisation. Remember that WFM is a journey, not a destination.

Consider the persona of your customer – frictionless interaction

If an electrician turned up at your home to install a light switch and they put it on the ceiling, what would you do? After your initial shock, you would have them move it to the wall and likely never use that electrician's services again. Technology should be no different. Place significant focus on the person using the solution to improve the overall employee experience. Design-thinking approaches and user journeys are a great way to achieve practical outcomes with technology. Consider what you are designing from a people perspective, and create journeys that define your requirements around this to ensure the solution is usable. Make the interaction frictionless.

Align the technology

Obtain IT alignment from the outset to ensure that your technology layer is aligned with IT standards (such as cloud, service management, security, availability, support, integration, architecture and so on).

It is easy to subscribe to a cloud-based technology without IT buy-in, but in the long term this may limit your organisation's ability to achieve its organisational goals and obtain the maximum value from its people. It's like with any project: without a plan and a strategy you run the risk of making a mistake.

What if you choose a technology that is end-of-life, does not integrate with your core HCM platform, has functionality that does not meet all the business needs or has an inability to scale? The best way to avoid this is to involve your IT team from the outset.

Get runs on the board quickly – the Agile philosophy

Implementation philosophy: Waterfall versus Agile. Agile is an incremental and iterative approach, whereas Waterfall is a linear and sequential approach. Agile separates a project into sprints; Waterfall divides a project into phases.

While this section is not to debate the pros and cons of each method, the Agile concept lends itself well to delivering outcomes where you can continually prioritise and check against your business objectives, benefits, adoptions and employee experiences. I believe the Agile implementation philosophy is becoming the norm when delivering projects. I am seeing more evidence of this across the vast number of projects I advise on.

Have the right team in place to ensure success

To achieve greater value in WFM, the right team is crucial. This stands true for your team, your product suppliers and your service providers. Make sure you choose your team in line with what you want to achieve and how you want to achieve it. Ask whether your team members are:

- quick to adapt
- good team players
- comfortable dealing with ambiguity.

If you have a strong governance layer in place to manage the process from the outset, you will be in a stronger position to achieve the desired business outcomes. All parties need to have a seat at the table to collaborate and achieve the agreed outcomes.

Measure and innovate

Traditionally at the end of a project the team disbands and that's the end of it. But if this happens, you have missed a vital step. Benefits need to be measured and the value of your investment needs to be understood. In the cloud world we are in a state of constant change, with continual new technology releases and enhanced functionalities available. Make sure any new functionality you implement remains aligned with and measured against your business objectives. Also ensure you keep your people front and centre, making space for them to explore their passions in alignment with the organisational objectives.

Along with technological advancements there will also be developments in people, process and business thinking that will guide organisations in how to best harness the new functionality. As this occurs we must adapt our approaches to keep pace, as the path to achieving greater value from people using digital technology continues to gain clarity. Chapter 9 of this book provides further guidance on this.

Top take outs

- While implementation is an important step in the process, it is only one step that your organisation needs to undertake. The 5-step workforce method looks at the *entire* WFM lifecycle.

- Top of mind in this methodology – however you enact it – is people.

- Follow the 'Tips for smarter implementation' given in this chapter when making decisions and adjust them to suit your business as required. Remember to consider all the tips for smarter implementation collectively.

Where to next?

Now I've introduced the 5-step workforce method, it's time to look at each step in detail. We'll unpack the key considerations to achieve value from WFM in your business. Are you ready?

CHAPTER 5

ALIGN

In the numerous WFM implementation initiatives I have been involved in or learned about, sometimes the leadership team has had a clear vision of the business outcomes they wish to achieve, such as increasing sales. At other times, the execution of these initiatives has been completed simply to solve an operational issue such as to automate the collection of time.

Bear in mind that if your senior leadership signs up to an increase in sales and your delivery team delivers a new time collection method to support payroll, your initiative will not be successful. It's important everyone is clear about what you are looking to achieve and how you are going to achieve it – from the top down and the coalface up.

HOW TO GET VALUE FROM WFM

The 5-step workforce method starts by aligning people to your organisational goals (see figure 5.1). We will also examine some of the considerations that are specific to WFM, enabling you to achieve value from an investment in WFM. This will, in turn, mitigate risk in any future steps you take to achieve that value.

Figure 5.1: Align

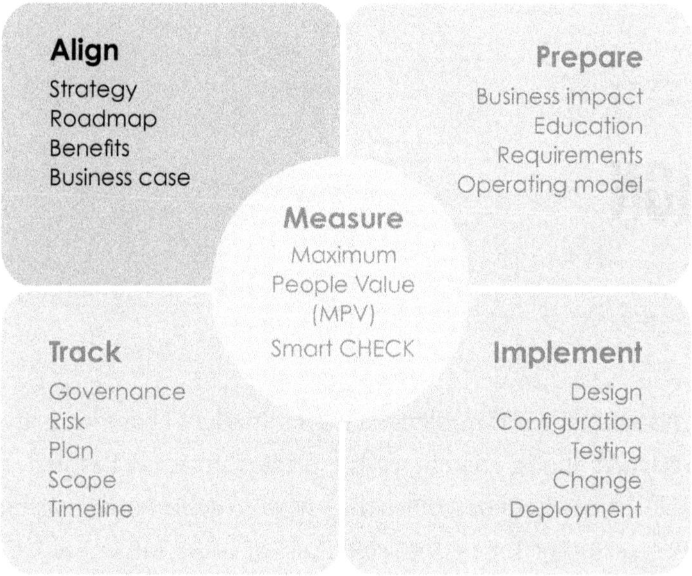

Align
Strategy
Roadmap
Benefits
Business case

Prepare
Business impact
Education
Requirements
Operating model

Measure
Maximum
People Value
(MPV)
Smart CHECK

Track
Governance
Risk
Plan
Scope
Timeline

Implement
Design
Configuration
Testing
Change
Deployment

ORGANISATIONAL GOALS

The first thing to consider when embarking on any WFM initiative is to understand your company's organisational goals. If you find your initiative is not aligned with the organisational goals, you need to ask yourself why this is the case. If you don't, a leader within your organisation is likely to ask you this question at some point.

Once you understand your organisational goals, you will generally find there are company initiatives underway that you are looking to align with from a workforce perspective.

Example: Dewi is CEO of an aged care facility. Her organisation's primary goal is to meet its residents' needs. Dewi decides to implement a WFM initiative to maximise the nursing hours per resident per day; this will bring the organisation closer to meeting its primary goal.

STRATEGY

A strategy to tie your organisational goals to your people is crucial. When you develop a people strategy, the benefits you achieve from WFM, along with the benefits you achieve from HR, need to be tied together. Without this strategy, you do not have a complete view of the people in your organisation. Organisations that consciously look at their people in a holistic manner have a greater chance of achieving better business value. This also leads to setting realistic expectations with your people in terms of benefits they will receive.

The strategy also needs to align with the technology you're planning to implement, to ensure that the people and processes within the organisation are aligned to produce a great experience.

Several organisations I have observed since releasing the first edition of this book have completed a technology transition, but still relied on the traditional people mindset and existing processes embedded within their organisation. A true digital strategy will take a human-centered design approach and reimagine process with a digital-first mindset – this will reap the greatest rewards for the organisation and people within the broader environment.

Let's look again at the previous example of the aged care facility maximising the number of nursing hours per resident per day. Meeting this organisational goal can also help to improve employee experience. Nursing staff are empowered to set their own availability for work, improving their work experience; and the AI algorithm maximises the effective rostering of staff. This brings together people, machines and algorithms both inside and outside the workplace. It's a move towards a new operating model to maximise value.

WFM is at the core of strategy as it aligns what people do, when they do it and how long they take to do it.

ROADMAP

As we have seen, WFM provides many benefits but there are several factors to consider in the approach to achieving them. The outcome of these considerations is a roadmap that examines the key areas such as benefits, people, process, technology, priority, timeline and return on investment (ROI).

With business priorities continually changing and the agile nature of business these days, roadmaps must be built in a way where they can pivot instantly and provide transparency on the impact of any pivots from the coalface through to the stakeholders.

The roadmap takes into consideration tips for smarter implementation to ensure success in any WFM initiative.

We'll now look at some areas for consideration that may be relevant to your organisation. I have focused on these areas as they can have significant positive or negative influences on your organisation's ability to achieve its business goals.

WFM organisational maturity

Different organisations are at various stages of WFM organisational maturity. I have seen organisations embrace people-related change at a rapid pace and adopt many of the WFM benefits as part of a single WFM initiative. The order of WFM maturity usually evolves as follows:

1. **Time recording** – electronically capturing start and stop times.
2. **Award interpretation** – feeding start and stop times to an electronic calculation engine that calculates the correct payment rules such as normal time, overtime, allowances and deductions.

3. **Rostering** – allocation of shifts and work on specific dates and times to people considering items such as coverage requirements, availability and skills required to complete this work.

4. **Forecasting** – applying additional rigour to the creation of a roster and allocation of work considering things such as sales volumes, patient intake, order of service to better determine the people requirements to meet demand and so on.

5. **Optimisation** – looking for further areas of optimisation within your workforce such as the optimal mix of casual and full-time staff working on specific shifts.

Some organisations are well positioned to complete holistic WFM adoption. The impact of change can be communicated, understood and adopted rapidly.

Be sure you understand where your organisation's maturity sits to make an informed decision when creating your roadmap.

Multifaceted organisations

Some organisations are made up of a collection of businesses and are therefore multifaceted. For example:

- a parent company may own three retail chains and a manufacturing organisation
- a council may be responsible for a contact centre, works management, health services and an entertainment facility.

Multifaceted organisations may not find a one-size-fits-all WFM process or solution and this is an important consideration when creating the roadmap. Each business and business area will have its own unique requirements. In the council example above, the four business areas (contact centre, works management, health services and an entertainment facility) may all require specific outcomes, which means each business area may need to have its own requirements and team rolling into the broader organisational initiative. We'll look at this in more detail in chapter 6.

EXPERT INSIGHT

Jason Averbook – CEO and Co-Founder at Leapgen – on roadmaps

Roadmaps are trickier than ever. Because of the speed, and because of the unknown, around some of the things that we're dealing with, I try to say there's a big difference between a roadmap and an active traffic control.

Active traffic control means I'm driving down the road and say, 'Hey, guess what, I see a traffic jam up here, I'm going to be guided to go a different direction.' The roadmap, on the other hand, might not even have the roads that I'm driving down correctly listed on it, because it's out of date. So, it's really important that organisations put some active traffic management in place. That way, there's someone in the navigating seat if, all of a sudden, we acquire a big company, or we end up in another pandemic around social justice, or we have a talent shortage.

Our old-fashioned roadmaps, looking three to five years ahead, are almost impossible now. If I asked you right now what this world of work is going to look like in three to five years, what would you say? If you can answer that question, you can give a prognosis, but I guarantee you're not going to be 100 per cent right.

Read the full transcript of my interview with Jason at: smartwfm.com/book

Prioritisation

When completing the roadmap, ensure that the organisational considerations are adequately represented and balanced. The roadmap will prove a valuable asset when moving into subsequent steps of your WFM journey.

As noted earlier, it is likely your organisation will undertake a multistage journey to reach an end state. I often complete roadmaps firstly by identifying the quick wins and foundational activities followed by enhancing operations and finally optimising operations.

BUSINESS CASE

The business case is a key outcome of the Align step. It complements the roadmap and often changes, or the impact of one will affect the other. The more effort you put into the business case, the more realistic the changes and costs will become to your organisation.

Implementation planning study

Some organisations complete an implementation planning study (IPS) at this point in the journey. The objective of the IPS is to take a deeper dive into your organisation to better understand how it operates, which will better inform the business case and provide further details for the roadmap. An IPS is analogous to a high-level planning and design phase for a project. It will generally look at potentially risky areas.

In my experience, an IPS is invaluable for multifaceted organisations and organisations with autonomous operating models to help them understand the complexity of the journey ahead.

Details of the IPS are further fleshed out in chapter 6.

People

People are at the centre of WFM initiatives and organisations place far more focus on people and positive experience today. This places a high emphasis on involving people heavily in your initiative, along with giving them responsibility to make decisions with appropriate support.

When you are in implementation mode, input from multiple perspectives is required. Consider the importance of 'backfill' with the critical roles on the project. In other words, when you take a person who works for your organisation and dedicate them to the initiative, you will need to find a suitable replacement for that person's substantive role. If not, you will be asking them to do their current job and whatever is expected from the project. This can result in poor quality delivery due to lack of time or burnout.

EXPERT INSIGHT

Anna Santikos – Director of People, Culture and Learning at Montefiore – on resourcing

Another big learning for us has been around resourcing. I think where we've given that greater consideration, we've seen more successful project implementations. Depending on the scope of the implementation, I think it can be very difficult to undertake that in a thorough way and give it the commitment and the consideration that it needs, if you don't provide enough resourcing and are trying to undertake this while fulfilling your substantive role.

We've experienced success where we've utilised internal resources – for example, seconding someone to a particular project to work through the implementation process. Utilising internal staff dedicated to the project has helped us make sure our systems are properly embedded.

Read the full transcript of my interview with Anna at: smartwfm.com/book

Be pragmatic and ensure you budget for this adequately when you are calculating your implementation and deployment costs. If you don't get this right, it can lead to frustration among your team members, and a less optimal solution.

Once you have deployed the solution, consider the support network required for it to operate: for example, implementing a team with detailed knowledge of the people, process and technology required to support the organisation. Also consider how many support staff you will require, and whether you will insource or outsource support.

Process

With an increased focus on improved people experience comes an increased need to provide localised processes. I'm not advocating that you build a process for every nuance in your organisation; rather, you need to ensure you understand the way of operating and get the process right. To obtain the business benefits you should follow a defined process and the cost of implementing the new process must be considered. Your organisation's WFM maturity will drive the cost of this change. At the outset of your initiative, you may think a single process is possible and, after obtaining more knowledge about your business, you might find you require more than one process.

Technology

Ensure you understand how many technology solutions will be required to deliver your end state and how these technologies will coexist.

In his report *HR Technology 2021: The Definitive Guide*, Josh Bersin notes that on average large organisations have 9.1 core talent applications.[1] With such a large number of applications, getting this right should be of high importance.

Consider technology that provides all your functions from a single application, or a technology layer that allows the user interactions to coexist across multiple technologies in a frictionless manner.

How many business cases?

If your organisation has a single operational model, it is likely a single business case will be put forward for the program of work.

Some larger multifaceted businesses essentially have multiple businesses within a business. Other businesses provide the same core functions to their clients but have different operating models across their locations. As people and people processes are at the heart of the business, different ways of operating can mean a few things or a combination thereof. For example:

- the business will continue to have different operating models
- the move to a standard operating model will require substantial change and adoption activities

---

1   Bersin, J 2020, *HR Technology 2021: The Definitive Guide: Everything you want to know about buying, implementing, and investing in HR Technology.*

- a number of operating models will be adopted.

Where there are different operating models, some organisations break their WFM initiatives into multiple business cases. While on the surface this may appear to prolong the timeline, there are benefits:

- each business case stands on its own merits
- there are fewer initial costs due to multiple projects starting at different stages
- you can get runs on the board quickly
- organisational change and adoption is spread over a period of time
- learnings from previous initiatives can be fed to future initiatives
- a repeatable process can be developed for future initiatives
- benefits and measures can be better understood each time around.

This approach can be particularly relevant for larger multifaceted organisations. It comes back to the fundamentals: understand the change, culture and mindset shift required to transform your organisation, and don't bite off more than you can chew.

FURTHER CONSIDERATIONS FOR THE ALIGN STEP

Let's take a look now in a little more detail at further considerations that are important in the align step.

Payment rules

Organisations often embark on a WFM initiative with the expectation that there will be cost savings as a direct consequence of the initiatives undertaken.

In some organisations, when EBAs are closely scrutinised or solution testing commences, it can be found that underpayments have been occurring for some time. In chapter 6 I provide some tips for dealing with organisational compliance issues, such as underpayments and overpayments that need to be resolved in the course of the WFM project.

Off-the-shelf versus bespoke solutions

The market has reached a level of maturity where it is becoming less likely that an organisation will require a custom-written bespoke solution. When choosing an off-the-shelf solution, traditional considerations come into play when you are selecting the right supplier to best meet your WFM needs. Some suppliers are better aligned technologically to one industry over another. Make sure you speak with other customers in the same industry with like requirements to help you mitigate any technology risk in this area. That is, be careful not to select a technology solution that does not meet your needs.

The importance of leadership

The core of why I wrote this book and the basis for the 5-step workforce method is that WFM projects are people projects, completed by the people for the people. With this in mind, to achieve the best results you need to own it and drive it.

In the past, businesses have traditionally focused on the Implement step. This is also the key area product suppliers focus on, as often everything else is outside their core remit. This is even more prevalent these days, as most product suppliers have venture capital driving their business growth and licence sales drive their valuation – their aim is to implement with a light touch and move onto the next product sale. This is not a negative, it's just a commercial reality. It's important to recognise this and deal with it when you are setting up your initiative because from a leadership perspective, you also need to focus on the other steps of the methodology.

Pilots

I once participated in a pilot conducted over a very short timeframe for a large global retailer. There was high senior leadership and end-user

'If an organisation is ready for change, has a culture of change and understands its WFM maturity, it can deploy rapidly and on-scale. I have seen successful global deployments across multiple geographies and sites take place in a number of weeks.'

—

Jarrod McGrath

acceptance due to a strong alignment of organisational goals and work-force goals. This resulted in an accelerated sales and implementation process benefitting both the customer and vendor.

Although many organisations conduct pilots, often pilots fall short of meeting the organisation's expectations. Generally, this is a result of any or all of the following factors:

- Organisational goals are not aligned with workforce goals, which results in a solution that does not solve the business pain.

- Team members are expecting a complete (end-state) solution, but the product supplier only builds a partial solution to save time and money. This results in the need for many manual processes and workarounds that deflate organisational and people's expectations.

- A small sample of 'easy' business areas is considered, but not the areas where the real pain is being felt.

Impact of supplier-provided templates

It is common for suppliers to provide templates for their customers to complete, because it allows the supplier to accelerate the configuration build required for an implementation. Types of templates might be used to capture people master data, locations of work, cost centre information, organisational roles and staff skills.

While this approach may keep the supplier cost down, it does not absolve you from the responsibility of completing the templates. In some respects, it transfers risk from the supplier to you; for example, risk of project delays due to non-completion, or the implications of making changes to the data in your templates. Make sure you understand the expectation the supplier has of you to complete these templates, and the outcomes that can be expected. There is more on templates in chapter 6.

Since writing the first edition of this book I have heard many customers express disappointment with supplier-provided templates. The templates are often confusing and do not take people and process – that is, the core elements of delivering outcomes in your business – into consideration. A recent customer noted that their biggest disappointment with their vendor was that they lacked understanding of the outcomes the business was looking to achieve (in fact, it did not care about the outcomes at all because they were 'not in scope').

Process and role changes to achieve business benefits

A defined process must be followed to achieve benefits. For example, if your organisational goal is to decrease operating costs, this may align to a workforce goal of a reduction in the amount of overtime worked. Your current process will involve various overtime approvals, including input from operational managers and administration staff. To deliver the benefits, you want to make your operational managers more commercially aware, remove the need for administration staff to input overtime and ensure the operational manager has increased visibility, along with giving them the skills to manage this effectively. In this case, the business process and role will need to change to achieve the outcome.

Another example of process change might be where your organisational goal is to give your people a better working experience. This may align to a workforce goal of enabling flexibility for your people to set their availability to work on weekends. The current process involves all staff being required to work on weekends on a rotational basis. Again, the process needs to change to achieve this outcome. In chapter 6 we will look at understanding the current state and preparation for change.

Duration of a WFM project

There is no easy way to gauge how long a WFM project will take to implement and deploy, but here are a couple of scenarios at each end of the spectrum to help put project duration in context.

For many organisations, however, timeline is not the key driver; rather, they focus on a successful outcome with low risk. Some organisations break the project into chunks by business area, complete a business case based on business area, and deploy based on business area. These initiatives can take several years to complete, but offer great benefits in terms of people experience and risk mitigation.

People, process and technology focus

Traditionally, let's say your team spent one-third of its time on people, process and technology respectively. Now that most solutions are based in the cloud, the technology activities should take significantly less time, so this allows the excess to be reallocated to high value-adding business activities. The depiction of approximate time allocation can be seen in figure 5.2. The additional time focused on people and process can theoretically be allocated to benefits such as improving employee experience, personalising the design and concentrating on business outcomes.

Figure 5.2: Time allocation – past versus present (cloud)

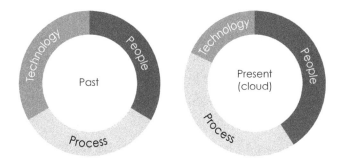

Over the past few years I have seen some examples of cloud-based projects where technology is still taking a large portion of the team's time. Often in this case – as noted earlier regarding supplier-provided templates – the technology vendor absolves itself from people and process. The consequence of this is that a lot of your team's time will be consumed to ensure the technical solution aligns with people and processes to deliver a paramount people experience. So, make sure your vendors are held accountable for delivering a solution that meets your business objectives. This situation can become even more challenging in organisations that have a large number of core talent applications.

Impact of industry type

Industry type has a significant impact on WFM initiatives. The major impact is the method of rostering and how this method affects your people's way of working. This also has flow-on effects to requirements and the product and service suppliers who are suitable to your industry. These areas are discussed in more detail in chapter 6, but here are some examples:

- **Manufacturing:** You require a fixed number of process workers on the morning shift, which runs from 7:00 am to 4:00 pm, five days per week. Shifts are fixed and repetitive.

- **Retail:** You are concerned about making sure you have your team members balanced to match the flow of customers into the store. Over the lunch period, customer numbers increase and additional staff are required. You require a pool of skilled casuals you can tap into quickly if team members call in sick. You require people with specific skills to greet the customer and personalise their experience. You require people with additional skills to complete the sale and gift-wrap the purchases.

- **Airline:** You need to consider which port the flight starts from, port closures, delays to flights and so on. This makes rostering highly dynamic and specialised due to minute-by-minute changes.

Industries where we traditionally saw WFM solutions being implemented included those with a high percentage of workers who are paid on an hourly basis. Representative industries where WFM has a high fit include manufacturing, public sector, transportation, mining, hospitality, education, retail, health, contact centre, construction, service, home health and security.

We are also seeing the emergence of WFM in white-collar and other industries. The reasons for this might include:

- people wanting to set their availability so they can spend time with their children
- the ability to handle contingent and gig workforces
- the ability to work remotely and in diverse locations
- the need to track staff for the purposes of contact tracing.

In chapter 6 we will look at how industries align to different types of rostering.

Digital transition versus digital transformation

Many organisations fail to realise the difference between transition and transformation. When this occurs, organisations can fall short of obtaining the business benefits they set out to achieve.

Digital transition is very technology-centric. As the name suggests, it transitions your current people and processes to new technology; for example, you might transition from an on-premises WFM product to a cloud WFM product to mitigate the risk of technology failure. A transition is fine, so long as that is what the organisation wants to achieve.

Digital transformation goes much deeper. It looks at the current business operating model and aligns people, process and technology to achieve the business outcomes. It empowers people to achieve organisational goals. For example, let's say your organisational goal is to transform the employee experience to attract and retain staff. If your people currently record their time on paper timesheets and receive their shift notifications via email, you might wish to achieve your goal by using WFM to record time electronically. This empowers your people to set their availability and notifies them of their shifts via an app on their phone.

True business transformation takes commitment from the coalface through to the stakeholder and should not be underestimated.

WFM – a journey or a destination?

The needs of your people and customers change regularly. Continual advancements in technology coupled with organisational maturity have an impact on your ability to adopt and change with WFM initiatives. WFM is an ongoing journey; you need to continually measure its effectiveness, and adjusting to change can harness great benefits for your organisation in the long term.

Also refer back to chapter 1 where we learned that the entire WFM lifecycle is ever-evolving.

Top take outs

- Understand your organisational goals as your first priority.
- Create a strategy and roadmap to tie your organisational goals to your people goals.
- Consider your organisation's WFM maturity.
- The business case ties the overall initiative together. One or many business cases may be required.
- Understand the journey your organisation is about to embark on from a people, process and technology perspective.
- Know that WFM is an ongoing journey, not a destination.

Where to next?

This step focused on setting the foundation in place to achieve value from your WFM initiative. We'll now take a closer look at what is required in your organisation before you commence your initiative to ensure its success with the Prepare step.

CHAPTER 6

PREPARE

Too often I see a disconnect between the business outcomes senior leadership is looking to achieve versus what is actually implemented. In extreme cases, large financial investments are made with little benefit.

I believe the biggest reason for this is that the organisation does not know what it needs to do prior to an implementation commencing. The consultants turn up to start an implementation with a statement of work that has some form of loose coupling to the business case. The consultants are ready to implement the technology and are hopefully well versed in the questions they need answered to configure the product based off their 'accelerators'. The organisation, on the other hand, has many unanswered questions.

Over the last three years I have continued to observe this, especially now that most vendors simply want to configure based off a business-completed template, with little understanding of business outcomes, processes or people.

The key learning here is that you must take responsibility for your own destiny.

WHAT YOU NEED TO KNOW BEFORE YOU START A WFM INITIATIVE

The Prepare step focuses on ensuring your business is educated and ready for the WFM transformation journey ahead (see figure 6.1). This includes understanding:

- your requirements
- what type of rostering models are needed
- which suppliers are suited to particular industries
- how to contract with suppliers
- the impact of change
- how your departments align
- the approach to deployment.

This chapter will unpack these key considerations to enable your implementation to be a success.

Figure 6.1: Prepare

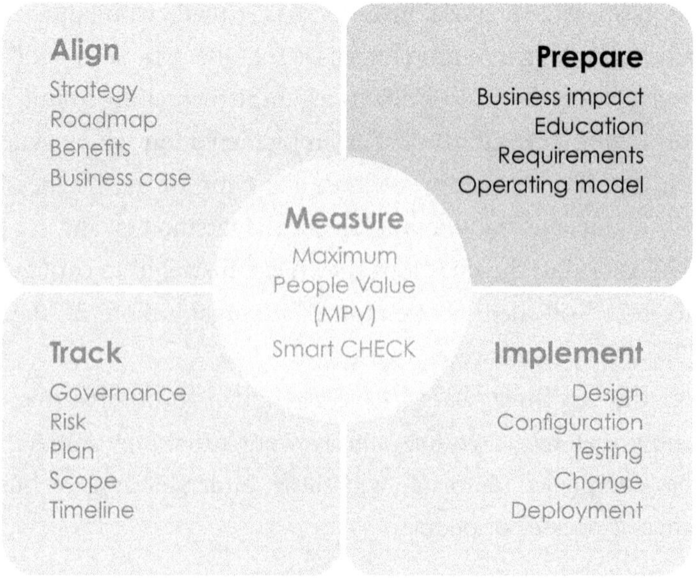

Align
Strategy
Roadmap
Benefits
Business case

Prepare
Business impact
Education
Requirements
Operating model

Measure
Maximum
People Value
(MPV)
Smart CHECK

Track
Governance
Risk
Plan
Scope
Timeline

Implement
Design
Configuration
Testing
Change
Deployment

UNDERSTANDING ROSTERING MODELS

Getting the rostering right in any organisation is key to business success. The more effectively you can manage your workforce to cover the work to be performed, the higher your returns will be. WFM has the ability to transform your business, providing you know what you want to achieve – in other words, you need to be prepared.

Rostering or scheduling?

In the 5-step workforce method there is no difference between rostering and scheduling – the terms can be used interchangeably.

In some organisations or across different suppliers, however, these terms mean different things. Rostering can be used to allocate workers over a block of time – for example, a day. Scheduling can be used to secure a worker to carry out a discrete activity that is completed during the day – for example, completing a service call.

Types of rostering

Before you embark on any improvement initiatives, it is important to understand that the method of rostering has a direct correlation to the way your operational workforce will function. This helps to frame the changes that will be required to deliver the business benefits. In my experience, rostering in organisations generally falls into four categories, which are described below. All industries start with shift-based rostering and some industries will build upon this baseline.

1. Shift-based

Shift-based rostering is the starting point for any organisation that rosters. There is a start time and a stop time for a shift. Often the shift will fall into a cyclic pattern, but it could also be an ad-hoc, once-off shift.

Example: Person 1: 8:00–4:00 pm, Monday to Friday. Repeated weekly. This is analogous to setting up a calendar entry in your favourite email system.

Shift-based rostering will allow you to achieve the following business functions:

- **Determine people's availability** – e.g. an employee can set a preference for availability to work on a given day/time.
- **Align skills to a shift** – e.g. you need one person on the shift to have a first aid certificate.
- **Complete shift swaps** – e.g. a person can swap their shift with another person who is available to work and has the required skills.
- **Capture start and stop times of shift** – e.g. a person starts and stops a shift on a given date and time.
- **Cost the time on the shift** – e.g. to determine which cost centre the shift cost should be allocated to.

Typical industries that use shift-based rostering include manufacturing, public sector, transportation, mining, hospitality and education.

2. Forecasting

Forecasting takes in additional factors to forecast labour demand for the future. These factors enable you to better align your people to the future demand on a particular day or time.

Examples:

In retail, forecasting allows you to align historical sales value by department to the number of people required to make the sales. Foot traffic is aligned to determine the number of people required to staff the store.

In health, forecasting allows you to align patient admission by department to the number of people required to treat patients.

In contact centres, you can align call volume with the number of people required to take the calls. For example, a product recall in a retail store relates to a predicted call volume.

Also refer to the section on labour standards below. It provides an overview of the process required to determine how long activities take, to help work out the optimal number of staff to roster on.

3. Work-based

Work-based rostering is based on the completion of jobs or projects. People are often allocated to teams/gangs/crews and complete multiple tasks to undertake a job or project at a specific location. These jobs or projects take place over variable periods (hours, days, weeks or months).

Example:

Team 1. Available 8:00–4:00 pm, Monday to Friday.
Repeated weekly.

Job 1. Monday: Fix damaged road.
Tasks: Pothole repair, fill cracks, seal coat.

Typical industries that use work-based rostering are construction and repairs and maintenance.

4. Route

Route rostering is based on the servicing of clients at given locations. People often work individually or in small teams and complete the same tasks for the same client repeatedly.

Example:

Service Provider 1 available 8:00–4:00 pm, Monday to Friday.
Repeated weekly.

Client 1. Monday: Domestic assistance.
Tasks: Prepare meal, shower, groom.

Typical industries that use route-rostering are home health and security.

Labour standards

Labour standards are a way to baseline the average time taken to complete a discrete piece of work – for example, the time it takes to serve a customer at a supermarket checkout.

To develop labour standards, time-in-motion studies and/or predictive analytics are completed to determine the overall time taken to complete a task or a group of tasks.

Labour standards are prevalent for the forecasting, work and route-based rostering models previously defined. The benefit of understanding labour standards is that based on the standard, you can better align and justify the required number of staff to the demand.

> **Example:** A retail store is expecting 450 sales over the 60-minute lunch period. One person can serve 45 customers in an hour. The standard shows that multiple staff are required to service the expected demand. The exact number of staff will be determined based on the average customer wait time the store is willing to accept, and any other factors the store considers relevant.

Roster optimisation

While labour standards help you align staffing to demand, roster optimisation helps you determine the optimal roster configuration to meet business rules. Roster optimisation may look like this:

1. Alignment of labour standards to required staffing.
2. Meeting obligations as defined in the EBA – for example, breaks between shifts, staffing requirements (senior and junior to be rostered together).
3. Meeting business objectives – for example, two seniors preferred to be rostered during the lunch period.

Roster optimisation is typically a complex analytical activity and requires specialist skills to complete. Not all product suppliers' software will enable this. These tasks are sometimes completed outside the WFM technology layer and the results are fed back into the technology.

Some organisations choose to implement all these items together, while others do it singularly or use a combination thereof. WFM maturity will impact your speed of adoption.

Centralised versus decentralised rostering

Centralised rostering is completed from a hub where all your roster team works for the benefit of the many locations within your organisation. Decentralised rostering is completed at specific locations within your organisation. Whether you complete centralised or decentralised rostering you will require people with specialised skills in your roster team to undertake this activity to drive the optimal results. There is no right or wrong answer when deciding upon a centralised or decentralised rostering approach; it's a matter of what works best for your organisation.

Here are some considerations when choosing what rostering type is right for your business.

Risk

Some businesses have functions and roles that are critical to successful operations. For example, in an airport you must have a luggage screener so passengers can clear security to hop on the plane, and there are commercial obligations you must meet. When you have a critical need, centralised rostering models can be attractive. You are able to ensure that all critical screening roles are filled across all your locations and you have full control over making quick changes if roles are not filled.

Skills

Decentralised rostering models require specialised skills to be spread across all your rostering locations to complete rostering. If you have a business where there is a high turnover of staff, you will have to continually educate new staff. This means you will have additional costs of education to cover, and you'll need to consider which methods of education are best, and so on.

Personalisation

If you have a well-skilled rostering team, you can personalise the rostering experience for your team. In decentralised models this is particularly relevant as the rostering staff will develop a personal relationship with their people, often leading to improved employee experience. On the flip side, if the quality of the rostering staff is not high, it can have the opposite effect on your employee experience.

ALIGNMENT OF REQUIREMENTS TO BUSINESS OBJECTIVES AND BENEFITS

It's important to first define the business objectives that overarch the high-level requirements. Requirements are more functional in nature and are often defined in a singular manner. For example, they may include the:

- ability to create a roster
- ability to create a roster pattern
- ability to cost a roster.

To understand what you are looking to achieve from a business objectives and benefits perspective, it helps to understand which high-level requirements are important to you. You also need to keep the people at the coalface firmly in mind at this stage in the process.

With the shift to human-centred design, detailed requirements are giving way to a stronger focus on personas, user stories and journeys supported by requirements.

Some WFM suppliers are able to provide a baseline set of requirements that you can take as a starting point. Your industry type is important when understanding your requirements, and specific requirements will be relevant to particular industries. For example, some industries will need the ability to allocate crews to jobs to fix a road in a service industry, while others will need to roster care workers to clients, enabling domestic assistance activities to be completed in home health care.

REPORTING AND ANALYTIC CONSIDERATIONS

Reporting and analytic considerations vary considerably. Here are my observations on some of the main things to keep in mind, along with some practical examples.

Operational and management reporting

Operational and management reporting enables user-based analysis, generally around day of operations or within a pay/roster period. Typical examples in WFM are:

- actual cost versus schedule cost reporting (such as normal hours, overtime hours)
- roster reporting (such as who is rostered to what shift, location of shift)
- effective roster reporting (percentage of time the roster meets forecast).

Metrics come into play with this type of reporting. For example, when production line labour cost approaches 95 per cent of budget, the operational manager should receive a notification.

WFM reporting is different to payroll or cost-accounting reporting in that it is available in real time. This allows a manager to make an informed decision to proactively address a scenario before or as it is occurring. The old saying comes into play: prevention is better than cure.

Predictive and prescriptive analytics

With the growing use of AI, machine learning and deep learning, we are seeing an increase in the value of predictive and prescriptive analytics. Predictive analytics uses data to predict the likelihood of a scenario occurring. For example, a person might have a history of taking a day off after they have worked a specific shift combination. To remedy this, the system may prescriptively suggest a change be made to the people making up specific shifts.

Specific data science roles that help identify and resolve trends that are occurring within organisations are becoming more prevalent, as noted earlier in the book.

Data

Data accuracy is imperative to enable decisions to be made based on what has really happened or is happening. The earlier example notifies management if labour cost approaches 95 per cent of budget. If the data is inaccurate, the cost might be at 105 per cent of budget when the decision is made. Driving a culture within your team to ensure your data is accurate and 'clean' is crucial to making correct decisions. Also refer to the section on data cleanliness in chapter 7, where I address this from an implementation perspective.

SUPPLIERS

It is common to use a combination of product and service suppliers to provide your overall solution. However, there are several important considerations that apply to selecting the right product or service suppliers for you.

When evaluating suppliers, don't just pay attention to *singular* business requirements as defined in a document, such as a request for proposal (RFP) or a request for information (RFI). Look at requirements collectively to ensure that *all* your collective business requirements can be met. This is also known as a user story. As noted earlier, taking a design-thinking and persona/process approach to this task is becoming common practice now. Consider a frictionless experience from a people perspective.

Industry considerations

Consider your supplier's fit to the industry that you work in; the terminology you use, the way you work, market trends and so on. Is the supplier aligned with your goals, benefits and requirements? Can the supplier play out and understand your business persona? For example, in the health industry, what does WFM mean for a nurse, or for a nursing unit manager?

Technology

Consider your supplier's technology alignment to the industry you work in. Different suppliers work more effectively in different industries. For example, one supplier may have a strong fit to retail but a low fit to health. Another supplier may have a strong fit to clinical health but a low fit to home-based health care.

EXPERT INSIGHT

Georgegina Poulos – Global Director People T2 and Global Retail Operations at Unilever – on choosing a supplier

Work with an awesome provider with a 'can-do' attitude. We've thrown our provider some curve balls along the way and it has been fantastic that they've been open to this. For example, coming into bushfire season in Australia we realised that, with more people working from home, we needed to do some emergency management. We knew which of our stores were situated in bushfire risk zones, but not people's homes. We wanted to know who would be at risk if emergencies struck. So, we created a new portlet in our system to allow team members to nominate whether they live in an area prone to bushfires, cyclones, hurricanes, floods, storms or earthquakes.

Read the full transcripts of my interviews with Georgegina at: smartwfm.com/book

Small-to-medium-sized business versus enterprise business

Some suppliers work better with SMBs, while others are a better fit for enterprise businesses.

Take the time to understand where your supplier's experience lies. In enterprise you may expect, for example, provision of strong governance, account management and onsite resourcing, to name just a few requirements. If you are choosing an SMB supplier to provide an enterprise solution, make sure they can meet your expectations and/or have a suitable partner to assist.

EXPERT INSIGHT

Cian McLoughlin – CEO at Trinity Perspectives – on supplier considerations

For a long time, when we invested in training our people, we were investing in product and solution skills. We weren't necessarily investing in the softer skills, because either we thought that they weren't as valuable, or we just assumed that people had those skills. The biggest surprise to me, I would say, in 10 years of conducting post-sales reviews with customers, is how frequently they talk about the people they interacted with from their chosen supplier and how critical a role those individuals play in them making a buying decision.

So, if a prospective customer is talking to three different vendors and, to a large extent, all three solutions can tick the boxes in terms of functionality and budget, how does the customer then make a buying decision? Well, they look to the people they have interacted with. 'How do they engage with us through the buying process? Do we like them, and do we trust them? Do they listen to us? Do they challenge us? Do they leave with insight? Who else have they worked with?'

This to me was on the one hand fascinating, but on the flip side disconcerting. Having spent my career in the industry not focused on those soft skills, it was a wake-up call when I realised their importance.

One of the key things that I'm recommending organisations do is ask themselves the question, 'How can we become easier to do business with?' Or, in the case of internal stakeholders, 'How can we become easier to interact with?' If you really want to answer that question, you actually have to go back and take a long, hard look at all of the touch points you have with your internal employees or your external stakeholders and customers, and say, 'Are these still fit for purpose?'

It can be hard to be easy to do business with – particularly if you're a larger, global business with established processes and systems, and hierarchies and fiefdoms that are trying to protect their own areas. This causes friction between the different areas of your business, which ultimately impacts the customer.

Now, we have new businesses emerging into markets who are operating in the cloud, and they're outperforming some of the more established players. That's because they're not beholden to all of these concepts, ideas and processes from another world. Some of the bigger players are having to do a heart and lung transplant on their own business to try to maintain that relevancy, and that's a hard thing to do at the best of times.

At the moment, there's so much change and uncertainty happening in the world that businesses are loath to embrace a whole lot of additional change and uncertainty. In this environment, the easier you make the interaction and onboarding process, the lower the barrier to entry and the more risk you take on yourself, the greater the likelihood that you'll get some business over the line.

If you can be the low-risk option, and help overcome that fear of change for prospective customers, then you're in a really strong position.

Read the full transcript of my interview with Cian at: smartwfm.com/book

Accelerators

Many suppliers will offer accelerators to facilitate your WFM initiative. Accelerators generally fall into the following three categories:

1. **Tools:** Methodologies, templates or scorecards used to inform your WFM initiative. This book is an example of a tool.

2. **Business led:** Used to capture information required by the product supplier to build the product. The supplier will expect you to complete templates, generally with minimal guidance.

   The templates are a way for product suppliers to keep their costs down, but they don't always inform you of the implications of what providing or not providing the data means for your business and their software. For example, say your data informs the design of your rostering model. The adopted design does not cater for your business to grow into additional geographies. To fix this will require significant reconfiguration and data realignment. This is an extreme example, but nonetheless a scenario that could occur.

3. **Technology:** Used as a pre-configuration or baseline to accelerate your configuration. The product supplier will expect you to adopt these pre-configurations as provided. Again, these pre-configurations are a way for product suppliers to keep their costs down, but they don't always suit your business rules.

It's important to understand what the supplier expectation is regarding variances and associated commercial implications if the accelerators are not suited to your business.

We will look further into accelerators and what they mean to your implementation from a business and technology perspective in the next chapter.

Roadmap and support

Understanding the supplier's roadmap and investment in research and development will help you make your decision about the right supplier to choose. If the supplier can show you a journey of where their organisation is heading, you will have more confidence in their ability to be with you for the long term.

It is important to understand items including:

- **analytics capability:** especially correlation and prediction
- **AI:** particularly machine learning and automation
- **people experience:** is the process frictionless?
- **omni channel:** is the platform capable of taking and processing multi-channel data in a seamless way, such as from social media, voice and the Internet of Things (IoT)?
- **cloud:** is the product 100 per cent cloud-based and built on a single data model?

The ability of the supplier and/or partner ecosystem to support the WFM solution is another consideration. Once you are live, you need confidence that any issues that arise will be dealt with promptly. WFM solutions are operational in nature and any downtime can have significant business impact.

Cultural fit

> '**I am a firm believer that a supplier cultural fit is critical for the overall success of a people focused initiative.**'

Jarrod McGrath

Is the supplier just trying to sell you a product or service, or are they really trying to understand you and your business? Does the supplier want to undertake a journey with you?

The impact of WFM across your business is far-reaching, and if you can't align on a cultural/emotional level, it places a question mark over your supplier's ability to work with you to undertake your organisational transformation.

Will the supplier be honest with you – and will you be honest with them?

Contracting

With the previous point in mind, when you contract with a vendor, especially in a cloud world, you are generally committing to a multi-year relationship with them. Make sure the contract is structured in a way that benefits you, and not the vendor. Can you break the agreement? Are there appropriate performance measures in place? Is your data accessible, and by whom?

Take responsibility for your own destiny

It has become very evident to me, over the last few years especially, that while the vendor takes responsibility for supplying the technology and configuring it to meet requirements, it is up to you as an organisation to understand your business. You must be clear on what your business wants to achieve, and ensure your vendor can create an experience that everyone will adopt to meet those business objectives.

Unfortunately, many customers think that once they choose a technology supplier the hard work is complete – that the solution will magically appear and be deployed into the organisation. Taking this approach is where I have seen the biggest failures over the last few years.

EXPERT INSIGHT

Jason Averbook – CEO and Co-Founder at Leapgen – on taking responsibility for your own destiny

If you go to the hardware store and buy a saw, does the storeperson come home with you and teach you how to use it? No. You just bought a saw. How do you use it? What do you do? You look at YouTube, or you look at the instruction booklet. It's the same thing with vendors.

Vendors make products. They are responsible for making sure their product works. The vendor is not responsible for making sure that your organisation works. They will not ask whether your organisation is mature enough to handle their product. That's not their job. So, the question is, do you have the skills within your team to do that, or do you need to hire someone to help you with the deployment?

There are a lot of organisations that have brilliant teams that are great at change. They're great at mindset building.

'You need to drive and lead the vendor, or you run the risk of getting a solution that isn't fit for purpose.'

—

Jarrod McGrath

They're great at helping map out futures. This is what you need within your team, before you even get to the technology.

Read the full transcript of my interview with Jason at: smartwfm.com/book

TECHNOLOGY

The next part in your preparation is to consider the technology.

IT strategy

Does your organisation have an IT strategy and are you aligned to it? Your IT department will have standards related to supplier credentials, security, availability, support, integration, architecture and so on.

With multiple cloud technologies it's essential to ensure the systems have an open API with easy ability to exchange data. It is easy to fall into the trap of assuming that data extraction will be an easy feat, but in reality this may not be the case. For example, let's say your learning management system (LMS) vendor says it is possible to extract its 'skills' information so the WFM system can consume it. On the surface, this seems straightforward. However, when it comes time to implement this integration you find out that each skill can only be extracted one by one with a single API call each time. Once the data is received, it needs to be stored somewhere and formatted prior to being imported to the WFM system. You can see how quickly this integration can became highly complex, and perhaps require a functionally rich middleware solution to successfully achieve the integration.

Your IT team will help you navigate this complex landscape, and are an integral part of the process. It's important to engage with them upfront during the preparation process.

Time capture

Today we have many options for time collection. Some of the common options are described below.

Biometric

With biometric time-keeping, generally a fingerprint representation is used to authenticate identity. This method is popular in organisations where prevention of time theft is a high priority.

Note: Often staff are concerned that an actual picture of their fingerprint is stored on the system. In my experience suppliers do not store an actual fingerprint; rather, a mathematical representation of the fingerprint is stored, which cannot be reverse-engineered to an actual fingerprint.

Facial recognition

The concept of this approach is similar to biometrics, with similar benefits. The main difference is that biometrics requires specific hardware (i.e. a finger scanner) whereas facial recognition can be implemented via software activation on most devices.

Mobility and geo-fencing

Mobile devices provide the ability to record information related to a shift. In addition, using a set of allowable GPS coordinates can define in what area a person can start and stop work using a mobile device. This is particularly useful for field service industries, and it enables employees to provide evidence of the location where and times when the work was performed. Other relevant information can also be captured such as job information, including materials used in field service industries.

Fixed devices

Fixed devices to record information related to a shift are beneficial when you want to ensure an employee's start and stop times are completed at the same place. These devices can be used for kiosk-type functionality such as costing transfers, applications for leave and viewing rosters. These devices are sometimes provided by the supplier or are available as commercial off-the-shelf devices (such as a tablet or iPad).

BUSINESS IMPACT

We covered the benefits of WFM in chapter 2. This section explains key areas of business impact in preparation for a WFM initiative that require closer attention.

Award interpretation

Award interpretation is core to many WFM initiatives. This is the process of taking an EBA and determining what will be configured. In Australia, the Fair Work Commission governs the agreements.

Can you configure directly from an EBA?

An EBA will define things such as rates of pay and employment conditions, such as hours of work, meal breaks and overtime. These areas are important to the overall interpretation of employee payments, but they do not define all the business rules. For example:

- If a shift runs over midnight, is the shift deemed to have started on the day the shift starts, the day the shift ends, or the day where the majority of the hours worked fall?

- If an employee starts work four minutes before the scheduled start of a shift, is the employee paid overtime, or is the start time rounded to the start of the shift?

In my experience, the configuration of the award is not the time-consuming part; most time is spent on the analysis and determining what will be configured. Do not underestimate the importance and the time required to successfully complete this step: it has a direct impact on the payments you will make to your people via payroll.

Some of the SMB solutions available on the market have pre-built EBAs. These generally have the baseline modern award configured. As a business owner, it is your responsibility to make sure you are comfortable with the interpretation and the payment of the EBA conditions.

EXPERT INSIGHT

Tracy Angwin – CEO at Australian Payroll Association – on reform and award simplification

There has been a lot of commentary recently about the need for payroll reform and award simplification.

The issue here is the volume and pace of change we've been seeing in recent times. Most employers are not even close to keeping up with the pace of change, particularly during the last 12 months.

We've experienced all sorts of changes during the pandemic that haven't necessarily been uniform. Nobody had time to think about how some of the solutions that both state and federal governments have devised will work in the pay office. So these new initiatives are devised, and the pay office is just expected to work out how to implement them. Sometimes that can happen fairly easily, and sometimes it can't. What I'd love regulators to understand is that every time there is change – whether it's IR reform or award simplification – it affects employers and their ability to pay people.

Payroll departments already have systems and processes in place. Every little tweak is a burden on the payroll office – it's death by a thousand cuts. Sometimes we'll go into an organisation and do a payroll compliance or process audit, and it's a dog's breakfast – but it's clear how that happens. We can see how organisations have implemented patch, over patch, over patch and ended up at a point where they need to stand back and look at the entire payroll function from beginning to end – because it's just spaghetti. And that's just because they've just been chasing their tail on all these small changes.

There's a lot of complexity that isn't often taken into account when changes are made from the top. For example, one of my client organisations has a handful of EBAs and a lot of long-term employees – so, a lot of people who have a lot of accumulated personal leave entitlements. Someone came up with an idea that if an employee has a lot of personal leave banked up, they could gift it to their colleagues – for example, new employees who may not have been working in the organisation for long enough to accrue leave.

Everyone – including the unions – thought it was a brilliant idea. However, coming back to the pay office, my first question is, 'Who's going to pay the tax? What are the fringe benefits tax (FBT) implications? Because essentially what's happening is the long-term employee is cashing out their leave. These are the types of questions that are not considered in the boardroom but that the pay office has to deal with.

In terms of IR reform, I think if we are going to do it, it needs to be a major change – not these little tweaks that we're constantly getting now, which I think is actually what makes it difficult for employers.

When people talk about IR reform, they're normally talking about awards and conditions of employment, and how we calculate what an employee's gross salary might be. I have a broader view that reform should include things that are governed by the Australian Tax Office (ATO) and state revenue offices. If we're going to reform employment, we need to look at the bigger picture.

Read the full transcript of my interview with Tracy at: smartwfm.com/book

Pay to EBA or site practice

When analysing your EBA, it is common to find that what is documented in the award is not what is being paid. In most situations when this arises, the site has made a localised interpretation of the EBA and pays to this. You will need to make a business decision as to whether to revert to the EBA or pay to site practice.

Sometimes senior leadership teams make a blanket statement that they intend to revert to an EBA. When the rubber hits the road, they find that current site practice is more generous and the risk of industrial action and change is too great. In these situations, the leadership team will often leave payment rules as per site practice. Remember that if you pay to site practice, the cost to implement and support site-specific agreements may increase.

At the end of the day, this is a business call. Make the call at this stage of the project and give the delivery team clear guidance. Chopping and changing with these decisions can be costly.

Who makes the interpretation?

It is important to understand who in your organisation is able to determine how an award is interpreted. There is no one size fits all here, as some of the following examples show. In some organisations:

- payroll makes the interpretation decisions based on timesheet data
- operations makes the payment decisions based on actual time worked
- payroll makes an initial assessment and clarifications are made by operations or payroll.

Don't leave your team in any doubt about who holds responsibility for these decisions. It's important that you determine who will be responsible for this now, as opposed to who does this in the future and who will make these calls on the implementation project.

Different interpretations of the same EBA

In many organisations the same EBA is in use across multiple sites and regions; however, it is common for interpretations to be different across the business areas. Simply put, the way one person interprets a clause may be different to the way another person interprets a clause.

Also consider grandfather clauses – that is, clauses that are carved out for historical reasons applicable to one or many employees. These are often highly localised and known by only a few people in the organisation. Working through this to reach an agreed outcome can be time-consuming.

What to configure?

Many EBAs have conditions that are not paid under normal circumstances. For example, there could be conditions for a certain group of workers, but your organisation no longer has this group of workers. Will you configure these rules or not? A business decision needs to be made at the outset of a project to ensure that expectations are set correctly.

Ensure you agree with this as part of contracting with your service provider. The costs of configuring non-used areas of an EBA can be considerable for both you and your service provider. Remember: design, build, test, deploy, support.

Underpayment and overpayment

When reviewing EBAs it is common for the business analysis to identify under and overpayments. I recommend establishing a treatment plan to address this early. Ensure transparency with your stakeholders and engage the relevant agencies where required.

Further reading

Don't blame software for wage theft

The adage of 'a good craftsman never blames his tools' is applicable to your WFM software. Don't blame the software you're using if you've failed to get your own processes in place or haven't configured your software to manage your varying EBAs.

Read the full article at: smartwfm.com/book

McGrath, J 2020, 'Good workers don't blame tools, so don't blame software for wage theft', *Australian Financial Review*, 2 March.

Award interpretation key learning

Award interpretations impact project timelines and budgets more often than any other area. Generally, the larger the organisation and the more autonomous its operation, the higher the risk associated with this. Many organisations establish governance committees or working groups at the commencement of the WFM initiative to work through these considerations.

Business/union consultation

Consultation with the relevant union(s) from the outset is imperative. Being clear with union representatives on the changes that are coming and keeping them abreast of this with regular communication is key. In many organisations it is important to get input from your industrial relations (IR) department; that is a conduit between your people and your leadership.

Compliance, stakeholder responsibility and industrial relations reform

Over the last couple of years we've seen several high-profiles cases in Australia involving underpayment and a lack of compliance with EBAs and workplace rights laws.

I feel strongly that we as business leaders must balance the needs of the workforce with the employer, unions, industry bodies and government, and also balance our stakeholder responsibilities.

There has never been a better time then the present to bring key bodies together to work for the greater good and provide a win-win outcome for all parties.

Further reading

Why a new approach to technology is crucial in IR reform
Workplace agreements struck up between enterprises, unions and staff rarely take into account the capability of company technology systems to implement them. It's time for this to change.

Read the full article at: smartwfm.com/book
McGrath, J 2020, 'Why a new approach to technology is crucial in IR reform', *Australian Financial Review*, 3 July.

People

Selecting the right sponsor is pivotal to ensuring your initiative's overall success. If you want to transform your organisation, choose a sponsor that has the drive and influence in the organisation to make this happen.

People in a variety of business functions, including operations, HR and finance, can take on the sponsor role.

In my experience, the greatest positive impact is when the role is adopted by operations and/or HR. People working in these areas tend to have the farthest reach into the operational parts of the business, which is where the changes take place.

Project manager

Arguably, this is the most vital role on the project. The role of the project manager (PM) will keep your ship pointed in the right direction every minute of every day. Make sure your PM understands their domain and can draw from real-life experiences to keep you informed, facilitate decision-making, set expectations and manage issues, risks and costs.

Engage the PM at the outset of the initiative and ideally consider getting them involved with the contracting process. This will enable a smooth transition to deliver the desired business outcomes and to ensure they fully understand the scope of work.

Change management

Organisations that conduct change successfully generally use a combination of the project sponsor, PM, operations and HR to collectively manage change. When undertaking a business transformation, credibility comes from those who are tightly coupled/aligned to those at the coalface. When you set up a two-way communication stream between these roles it makes for very effective and clear messaging between all parties.

We'll learn more about change and the various roles and experiences in chapter 7.

Project roles and skills

Selecting the right representative team on the project is instrumental to the overall success of your WFM initiatives. You are dealing with people, their emotions and their livelihoods, so I would encourage you to have your brightest minds working on delivering the initiative. The key touchpoints include:

- **Operations:** The methods of operating will likely change with the introduction of WFM. For example, in a service industry, the way time is collected on completed jobs may move from manual to digital. In other organisations, there may be two business types: service and manufacturing. To understand your business operating models you require representation from each of the operational areas to help shape the future way of operating.

- **Finance:** WFM initiatives are generally looking to improve the accuracy of costing to enhance financial forecasting. It is important you have strong financial representation, particularly from a cost-accounting and reporting perspective.

- **Payroll:** Times that are collected are award-interpreted producing hours, which are fed to payroll for payment. Ensuring your payroll team is involved will help reduce any risk associated with pay results.

- **IR:** WFM projects will often identify pay anomalies or change the way of working. There can be clarifications or changes required related to the EBA. Having IR reps involved from the outset will help drive these processes and mitigate risk.

- **HR and senior leadership:** Your people will be affected from a number of perspectives: the way they work, potential redundancies, efficiency improvements, repurposing, changes to job descriptions, downsizing and so on. Having HR and senior leadership involvement will help make the transition smooth.

- **Your customers:** The impact on your customers should be positive. Your staff should have less need to focus on administrative tasks and be able to concentrate more on personalisation.

Project role time requirements

There is no simple answer to the question of time requirements for each role in the WFM project. It depends on a number of factors such as the size of your organisation, number of staff available by business area, which roles take on which project function and so on.

The most important thing to realise is that many areas of your business are impacted by a WFM project so to achieve the best outcome people will need to work together. Freeing up the time of these specialists is often one of the greatest challenges to achieving your outcomes, but also the most valuable.

Business roles

The greatest changes are seen in the operational area of your business, focused around operational and payroll improvement:

- **Operations:** The impact is seen from a tactical and strategic perspective. Tactically, operations managers are empowered to set rosters, complete time approvals and manage leave, to name a few affected areas. Strategically, operations managers have greater analytical visibility and understanding of what their team members are doing from a staffing and financial perspective. This enables them to become more commercially aware, develop their team and spend time on customer experience improvements.

  Having operations managers become more commercially aware has greater benefits in your organisation as this can lead to time being spent driving a greater sense of purpose and ownership for the team members. This then has a direct impact on the operations manager as they can develop skills that allow them to grow from a professional and personal perspective. Ultimately, this can result in your operations managers becoming more business-like in nature.

- **Payroll:** WFM initiatives result in the automation of hours calculation for people's pay and the automation of hours transfer to payroll. This has a direct impact on payroll, allowing them to concentrate on value-adding activities.

People key learning

In many organisations, payroll completes a lion's share of the tactical activities that operations managers often undertake in a future state. These organisations find they have substantial change and transformation associated with the implementation of WFM. This requires helping operational managers understand the importance and benefits associated with completing work under a new way of operating.

IMPLEMENTATION CONSIDERATIONS

To wrap up this chapter on preparation, let's consider these final implementation considerations.

Global, regional and local influences

Larger organisations will work across countries and regions. This will result in some practices that may need to be adopted and/or modified. For example, a particular location may have a public holiday on a defined day; some regions may have cultures that don't work well together; some countries might have differing business goals based on societal maturity.

Your ideal goal is to adopt global organisational standards where possible, but understand that regional and local influences will come into play. The more you localise, the more support you will need to give to the solution. Ask yourself two key questions:

1. Are we localising because there is a true business need to do so?

2. Are we able to redefine our business rules to look for standardisation here?

Recall the fundamental requirement to not bite off more than you can chew. On the surface, it may seem like a clever idea to standardise, but the reality to make this happen may be different. Be realistic.

Understanding the current state

Implementation of WFM will often require a change from one operating state to another. If you are going to achieve business benefits, you will be required to adopt a particular way of operating. Understanding the current state enables you to understand how great the change required is, and can help inform the design. The Implement step begins with the concept of a survey to help you understand the current state.

For example, the product supplier wants to understand your requirements so they can design the technology layer. You want to understand the global, regional and local influences to inform the design. Not understanding your current state can delay the answers to the questions the product supplier has asked while you obtain the answers, and this can result in tension between you and your supplier.

Preparation for organisational change and adoption

The more you know about your organisation, the greater the chance the changes will be adopted. Success will be driven by your organisation's commitment to understand, own and drive change. When you get this right, WFM initiatives will be embraced and adopted.

EDUCATION AND METHODOLOGY

WFM and its functional components, such as rostering, are not a formally recognised discipline or skill. Most people who work in WFM end up doing so due to circumstances. There are a number of technology courses (from suppliers) that define how to access, design and configure a WFM solution, but they don't explain what this means to your organisation.

Some private institutes and associations have been looking to bridge this gap, but none have succeeded as yet. For me, the real point is that the WFM discipline is yet to be adopted by universities and certified education institutions.

'It is important to understand the current state prior to commencing implementation. Many WFM initiatives stall or don't deliver the desired business benefits when the current state is not understood to inform the change.'

—

Jarrod McGrath

Why do I call this out? It really comes back to the key reasons I wrote this book – to increase WFM awareness, look at WFM through a business lens and provide a repeatable, practical methodology. Once you have this, you increase your ability to give the greatest value back to your organisation and the people who work in the area of WFM.

If you are looking to upskill and improve your digital WFM, don't forget that as a valued reader, you have access to the Smart WFM Academy and Microlearning Suite linked to this book. I am passionate about raising the bar and sharing the knowledge that I have been fortunate to be gifted over the years. I hope you benefit from this learning program.

Find it at: **smartwfm.com/book**

Top take outs

- Organisations need to take responsibility for their own destiny.

- Understand the rostering model(s) that are required.

- Will rostering be centralised, decentralised or a hybrid?

- It's never too early to start cleaning data. The cleaner the data, the better informed your decisions will be.

- Many factors influence the selection of a supplier, especially industry fit, cultural fit and ongoing product investment.

- Supplier accelerators can push the responsibility of the implementation and achievement of business outcomes back to the organisation.

- Award interpretation is a high-risk area; don't avoid it, simplify it or push it to the side.

- The internal investment in people to ensure success of a WFM initiative is key to delivering a successful outcome.

- Understand what flexibility you can allow across countries, regions and locations.

- Create organisational awareness and build education from the beginning.

- Process change will be required to deliver the outcomes.

- Investing time to improve your understanding of digital WFM will help you bring the maximum value to your organisation.

Where to next?

This chapter focused on business and supplier readiness to enable a successful implementation. We now move on to Implement, which focuses on requirements, technology implementation and the business change that is about to occur in your organisation.

CHAPTER 7

IMPLEMENT

Determining the business outcome you are looking to achieve is in many respects the easy part. Working out what you need to do in your organisation to achieve the outcome is often the harder challenge. Far too often I have seen a sales process finalised with the implementation literally starting the next day. This quick start is fine, provided you are prepared for the task at hand. In my experience, the preceding step is rarely fully completed

WHAT YOU NEED TO KNOW TO ADOPT WFM

This step focuses on making sure your people, processes and technology are optimally aligned so that everyone in the organisation knows what to do and when to do it (see figure 7.1).

I still see too many organisations failing to achieve the right balance between people, process and technology, which leads to less-than-optimal business outcomes.

This chapter will help you get it right. It examines areas for success including understanding how the organisation is currently operating; creating standards and rules for implementation; understanding the scope and plan; determining which methodologies will be used; planning how the delivery will take place, and how change, training and support will be enacted to support the deployment. In other words, this chapter unpacks the key considerations to ensure the implementation is a success.

Figure 7.1: Implement

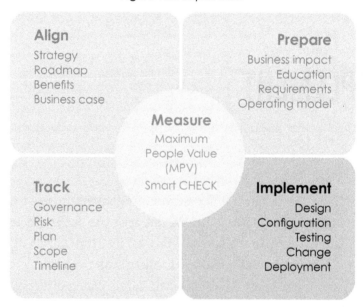

SURVEY

The more information you have about your organisation, the better prepared you will be for the changes ahead. WFM projects have a significant impact on the operations of your organisation. Over time, it is common for operations managers and their staff to develop their own ways of working. This is not a bad thing, but this diversity can influence the requirements, design, change and adoption associated with the implementation of your new solution.

An ideal way to find out more about your organisation is to complete a structured survey prior to commencing the implementation. The more knowledge you have, the more informed you will be in the upcoming decision-making process and this will accelerate time-to-value.

Note: you may also complete the survey as part of the Align step. It is never too early to collect this information.

Key areas of required business insight to consider for the survey are discussed below.

Sites and locations

For each of your sites, understand who your key contacts are in operations, HR, payroll, finance and IT. In larger, multifaceted organisations, variances are common, so be sure you know who can support you to obtain the required information. It may seem elementary, but knowing who to contact at a site to help you work through implementation items is invaluable.

Here are some questions you need to consider:

- *How many sites are there?* This will help you to work out how many operational methods there are and, therefore, the extent of the changes required.

- *Are the sites spread across multiple geographies?* This will help inform you of the requirements to support the solution.

- *Does your organisation own the site(s) or are you subcontracted to work there?* This will help determine the physical and technology access protocols you may be required to abide by.

- *What technology does each site run; what browser; what is the network speed?* This will have an impact on the desktop/mobile technology versions that you can use to run the software.

- *What HR/WFM applications does each location currently run?* This will help decide things like how many integrations will be required and the quality of data.

The answers to these questions will provide relevant input in upcoming decision-making.

Employment type

It's important to understand the basis of employment for your people at the sites and locations. Are the staff:

- full time
- part time – casual
- contractors/gig workers
- seasonal
- salaried
- self-managed teams?

How many people fall under each of these different employment types?

These breakdowns will inform operating models. For example, will the onboarding process be the same across employment types? Will the payment conditions be the same across employment types? Do you need to communicate change differently to each group of employees?

Current method of rostering

Understanding how the location sets rosters will inform the future state. For example, a hospital may have multiple locations: the emergency department, radiology, operating theatre and so on, and they may all roster in a specific way.

Award catalogue

Understanding your awards, the history of them and the way they are interpreted can be one of the greatest challenges and risks associated with any WFM implementation. I spoke in the last chapter about award interpretation and how awards are not one size fits all. This section should be read in conjunction with the previous chapter.

This step in the survey process is a key step to mitigating many of the award risks that have been previously identified. You would be surprised how few organisations are able to provide a full list of agreements they have in place, across which sites/locations they are applicable, who is responsible for interpretation and what the review date is for each award.

When you engage your technology vendor, they will ask questions to enable configuration of their products. If you are not able to answer these questions promptly, it can place significant stress on people, timelines and scope.

Time-collection methods

Understanding your current process of time collection is important to determine your baseline: paper, electronic or a combination of both methods.

Sample artefacts

Obtaining sample artefacts is a great way to capture a current snapshot of your business operating model. I've always been a believer in 'look and learn'. One big advantage of collecting these artefacts is that it enables you to see what data is being collected. You often find things outside your current understanding that are integral to the business operating smoothly. As these systems are operational in nature, carefully consider the implications of any changes.

> **Example:** Thompson Road Repairs finds out that its gangs are using different materials when repairing the road. Information about which material and how much of it is used in each repair is being collected on the same form the employees are completing their time entries on.

The implication here is that you can't just remove the timesheet form as the materials information being collected is still required to inform procurement activities.

The earlier in the process you identify scenarios such as this, the quicker you can find an optimal resolution or workaround.

Data cleanliness

Data analysis will help determine which sites and locations are more thorough and diligent than others. For example, are you capturing accurate actual data once, or do you have to manipulate the data to represent actuals? The answers to these questions will help drive subsequent reporting requirements and business KPIs.

With the emergence of AI and predictive algorithms, the cleaner the data the more accurate predictions will be. If your WFM system is predicting late arrivals to work with 95 per cent accuracy and the data to predict this is out by 15 minutes every day, the prediction will also be out.

Knowing which sites, locations and people develop and promote clean data will allow you to propagate these good habits throughout your organisation.

Survey key learning

Those organisations that complete the survey process thoroughly lay a solid foundation for their future operating model. Conversely, those organisations that assume they know everything already are at greater risk of building on a shaky foundation. It is challenging work to complete this type of thorough analysis, but the results speak for themselves. You will find yourself referring to this key information over and over during the process.

DETAILED REQUIREMENTS

The previous two steps in the workforce method have a strong focus on the alignment of your organisational goals to your workforce goals. Now you also know from the previous section the importance of understanding how you currently operate.

At this point, you can take your big picture and overlay it with the current way of operating to create your new future work model.

I believe this is a crucial step in any project as it allows the 'rubber to hit the road'. Everything you do from this point forward will be fundamentally impacted by these decisions. While you are still in the implementation stage, you can make changes to the design using information at hand, but once you go past this step, any changes to requirements may have a fundamental impact on the benefits your organisation will receive and when it receives them and the overall costs to deliver. These requirements will influence your operating model, which benefits you can deliver and how quickly you can deliver them.

Requirements baseline

At this point in the process you have enough organisational knowledge to create a requirements baseline. The requirements are informed by items such as different rostering models, award conditions and operating objectives that we previously spoke about.

These requirements should always be aligned to the organisational goals.

Personas, user stories and journeys

Business personas, user stories and journeys are the logical starting point for your design team. Human-centred design approaches enable you to reimagine your process and consider the convergence of people, technology and the environment to determine the optimal people experience.

Process building blocks

Once you know your requirements and have your personas, user stories and journeys mapped out you can define a process to meet the expected experience.

Figure 7.2 shows an example employee lifecycle building block framework that you may want to use as a starting point to build your people processes.

Figure 7.2: Example employee lifecycle building blocks

Human capital management People strategy	WFM People operations	Payroll People compliance
Talent planning and attribution	Interpreting payment rules	Payroll policy
Recruitment and placement	Forecasting and rostering	Manage payroll components
Onboarding and compliance	Track time	Manage data input and validation
Learning and growth	Exception management	Payroll processing, distribution and statutory compliance
Performance optimisation and flexible work practices	Approvals	Payroll accounting
Career and succession planning	Pay period end	Reporting and analytics

Traceability

Traceability is a way of ensuring that you are meeting your business outcomes and mitigating the risk of the technical solution failing to meet the business objectives and requirements.

BUSINESS IMPACT

From a business perspective, don't rely solely on third parties to completely own the implementation process. There are a few reasons for this:

- You ultimately need to take responsibility for your own destiny.
- Your people will only truly accept and respect a solution that is driven by you – they don't want to be told by product suppliers or consultants what to do.

- You are going to change the way you operate so you need to understand what this means.

Often I see organisations using a combination of an external supplier such as Smart WFM for their WFM experience and product configuration, coupled with the organisation's deep business knowledge. The inputs and skills from both are highly collaborative and can lead to a higher quality outcome – maximising people and organisational value.

PROCESS

The amount of process change depends on your starting baseline. At one extreme, you could be starting with paper time collection and rostering processes which you are digitising and streamlining. At the other extreme, you could have an existing WFM solution with efficient processes that you are tweaking to drive further efficiency improvements.

Most organisations will be undertaking process change. You will only achieve the business benefits if you follow the process.

TECHNOLOGY

We're back now to a discussion on technology. This time we're interested in where it fits in the Implement step.

Configuration standards

Prior to commencing the configuration of any solution, you'll need to understand what standards your product supplier is going to adopt to build the solution.

The larger and more multifaceted your organisation, the more important this becomes. If you share too much configuration, a change to one site's requirements in the future may result in changes of configuration to another site – even though its requirements may not have changed. This can result in a regression test, which can be costly in terms of integrity, time and money.

Consider configuration standards in a top-down manner:

- **Global** – what standards will be adopted that apply across the entire solution? For example, naming conventions, costing rules and reporting.

- **Regional/business unit** – what standards will be adopted that apply at a regional level? For example, the EBA set-up and time-collection processes.

- **Local** – what standards will be adopted that apply locally? For example, rounding rules, site-based allowances and deductions and the rostering set-up.

Not making these considerations prior to commencing configuration can have a significant impact on your WFM solution's ability to flex and meet the demands of changing business requirements.

Enterprise architecture

Understanding where the WFM solution fits into your organisation's overall enterprise architecture will help determine the boundaries and crossover points with other applications. From a WFM perspective, there are several components that make up an enterprise architecture. Let's take a look at the main components.

Applications architecture

Which applications exist in the organisational landscape? Is your organisation part of a group entity where there are standards in place around applications that should be followed?

WFM has strong integration with HR, payroll, finance and, in some industries, job management and forecasting systems. There are many permutations of which system functions are completed in which systems to deliver an optimal solution. Figure 7.3 gives a simplified sample architecture from a WFM systems perspective that could be tailored to your organisation's unique situation.

Figure 7.3: Sample applications architecture

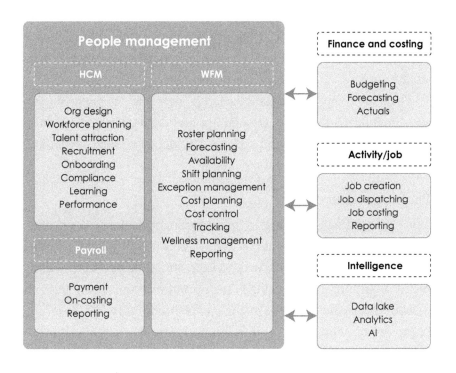

If you find you are integrating your systems, the four main design questions I see debated are:

1. Which system will leave be completed in?

2. Which application will be used for mobility?

3. Where will self-service be completed?

4. Where will award interpretation be completed?

My recommendation is to deal with all these questions at the outset of any initiative. When determining the answers, ensure you consider what this means to the person at the coalface and whether the system has been built by the product supplier to deliver those specific coalface requirements. You need to understand which functions reside in which system. WFM systems by their nature are designed for people at the coalface.

Technical architecture

Understand your technical requirements early in the implementation process. Engage with the IT team to identify any standards they have in place and work with them to design an optimal operating technical architecture.

There are many considerations across areas such as security (data and functional), network, servers, application, integration, desktop and performance – and organisational considerations such as procurement and ongoing support.

Platform architecture

Some product suppliers are building their applications on an open application programming interface (API). This means that it is possible for you to send and receive data to/from almost any complementary platform. In turn, this is seeing best-of-breed platforms being selected to achieve specific functions such as onboarding, core HR, rostering, payments, pay and so on.

For further information refer back to chapter 6.

Mobile architecture

Mobile-first systems are expected today. Some suppliers excel at this and others struggle. Many organisations are trending to bring your own device (BYOD) solutions. This means there are a myriad of mobile operating systems that the technology needs to be capable of working on. Not every product supplier has their application suite working seamlessly across all device technologies. Here are three key things you need to consider from a people experience perspective:

1. If some devices are not capable of running the WFM application, how do you achieve a single process across your organisation?
2. Do you now mandate that some functions need to be completed on another technology such as a PC?
3. Are multilingual capabilities available across the mobile devices/ operating systems?

It's important to understand whether you are in this situation early in your implementation, as working through the resolution can take some time.

Data architecture

The greater the number of systems and technologies in play, the more important data architecture becomes. Ultimately, the data that resides across your WFM and broader HCM solutions will be required for operational, management and predictive analysis. It becomes critical to understand where data resides, where its source is and which systems require it at which frequency.

Time-collection architecture

An area to consider early in your WFM implementation is the installation of time-collection devices. Technology today provides far greater flexibility for this, via wired ethernet, Power over Ethernet (PoE), satellite and mobile networks.

Some organisations have staff working on client sites under contract. For example, a cleaning company may supply staff on a permanently contracted basis to a hospital. In this case, the hospital may not allow the cleaning company access to their network to collect time information. While there are several options for the cleaning company to solve this challenge, working through the permutations of options and coming up with the most efficient, cost-effective answer may take some time.

Deciding where to install the device may also need some detailed consultation. In heavily unionised sites you may need to go back and forth between the parties to determine a suitable location. Take a situation where the placement of a time-collection device has been deemed to negatively impact pay – for example, if the time-collection device is moved from the front gate to the production line, employees' clock-on time will start later, potentially affecting their pay.

'You need to select a project team whose members have an ability to think objectively and consider the overall greater good of their organisation, their people and their customers. People are at the core of these initiatives, so unbiased people-focused team members are key.'

—

Jarrod McGrath

THE PEOPLE INVOLVED IN THE PROJECT

It is people who drive the success of your organisation's WFM implementation. In this section, we place an emphasis on the people considerations from a project perspective.

Project team

WFM works across a number of departments within your organisation. There is a high chance you will be implementing process change to achieve the desired business outcomes.

When taking a closer look at your operational models, you often find subject matter experts who can become an integral part of the project team. These experts are generally very passionate about what they do, and they can have an extremely positive influence on future operating models and how well people adopt the changes.

Anecdotally, I often find that when you staff your WFM project with business subject matter experts, the credibility and acceptance within your organisation is greater. It's always better to hear from someone who has learned from real experiences within your organisation than from an external consultant.

Project roles

For many project team members, it is often the first time they have worked on a project of this type. Once you commence the Implement step, project team members require clear direction on the role you expect them to play in the project. Ensure the team members understand their responsibilities.

Organisations should consider putting KPIs in place to help drive the right outcomes and behaviour of project team members. In some circumstances, I have seen the role of the project team member become redundant at the conclusion of the project. In these cases, having a KPI attached to an incentive, often financial, is critical to ensure a successful outcome.

Project team education

It is a good idea to have some form of induction planned for your project team. Help the team members understand what the objectives are for the project, their roles, how to handle issues, risks, time-recording requirements, work hours, site access, remote access, weekly reporting and so on. A lot of time can be wasted if these items are not covered before the project gets underway.

External consulting teams

Most WFM projects have external consulting teams that contribute to the project's overall success. The closer and more collaboratively you work with these teams the better. It's important to realise that everyone on the project is there because they have something of value to add. Take time to understand the background, passions and specific skills of each member of your project team. It's rare you don't make new friends and gain new knowledge in these circumstances.

I have seen situations where the project teams end up working in an 'us' and 'them' scenario. If you find yourself in a position where this is happening, ensure all the parties address this openly in a constructive way. Project governance input may be required at this point.

Remote teams

Remote work is now common practice, thanks partly to the global pandemic necessitating it and proving it is possible. Video conferencing has matured, and cloud-based collaboration tools are mainstream. People with the right skills can be formed rapidly into teams to solve specific business problems.

Scope and plan

Prior to commencing the implementation and bringing on board the delivery team, make sure the scope is clearly articulated and understood by everyone.

METHODOLOGY

> The 5-step workforce method is in no way meant to replace traditional or supplier methodologies. It is designed to complement existing methodologies by providing experience, knowledge, anecdotes and examples of what I've seen occur in organisations. You can plug and play any of these learnings into any methodologies.
>
> The 5-step workforce method is designed to bridge the gap between existing methodologies and the additional nuances that come into play with WFM initiatives. There may be aspects I have not documented that are relevant to your WFM initiative. Feel free to adapt the method to your organisation's particular circumstances.

Traditional methodologies

I refer to traditional project management methodologies as being the likes of PMBOK and PRINCE2.

The key thing to realise is that these methodologies are generic in their nature. They don't take into consideration supplier methodologies or the nuances of rolling out WFM. A notable example of this gap is the parallel testing process, which we will look at later in this chapter. I do not suggest you discount traditional methodologies; in fact, the governance and thinking they provide is very rigorous.

Supplier methodologies

Many product suppliers have their own implementation methodologies.

The important thing to note is that these methods generally place a stronger emphasis on the product implementation process, not the broader implications on your business outside the product, such as business change and adoption. You may need to demonstrate you have followed these methods to obtain ongoing vendor technical support.

Agile and Waterfall

Consideration of Agile versus Waterfall delivery methodology is also important. Refer to chapter 4 for more on this.

Adopting Agile design-thinking delivery techniques mandates that you consider your digital transformation from a people-first perspective, allowing you to ideate and get runs on the board quickly.

We use design thinking extensively in our digital transformation projects at Smart WFM, and the results speak for themselves. Processes are designed with people's experience at the heart and soul of the new operating models.

DATA

WFM systems rarely operate in isolation. There are typically two other integration points – the HR and the payroll system (refer to figure 7.3, which depicts a sample application architecture). It is more common for there to be other systems also sending/receiving data to/from WFM. For example, retail has point of sale (POS) and forecast sales; service organisations have job management; and the health sector has patient intake demands.

Data alignment across these systems for any end-to-end testing can take considerable time and effort to coordinate. It's important to get your head around the data requirements early and get a good handle on what is required to align the data. Understand the effort it takes to obtain/create data and to refresh data at a point in time – for example, understanding the backup and restore criteria. Take copies of data at appropriate points in time so you can restore it as required to complete your testing process.

As noted earlier in this chapter, data cleanliness is even more important with the introduction of AI and machine learning. You can only measure and learn from what you collect. You can only learn correctly if you learn based on clean data. This is no different to a student being taught the wrong thing by a school teacher.

Historical data migration

There are two main types of WFM data: historical time data and rostering-related data.

I have rarely seen historical time data migrated when an organisation is moving to a new WFM platform. Often discretionary decisions are made that implicate the payment results. Not knowing what led to these discretionary decisions and why they were made can result in award-interpreted hours being different between the old and new systems (manual or electronic), resulting in reconciliation anomalies.

It is more feasible for rostering data to be migrated to a new system in terms of the baseline rosters that are required. To do this, import and export functions at the technology layer are required. Ask yourself: will rosters in the future system be the same as the current system? If there is a difference, migration may not be possible.

Testing

Testing is a critical activity in any project. In particular, the testing of award-interpreted hours and its integration with payroll to produce the correct results is of the utmost importance. In fact, if this step fails, the result can be almost catastrophic, with people not getting paid correctly. This kind of error can directly impact people's livelihoods.

At the testing point of a WFM project it's often found that what has been configured works according to the documented EBA, but it does not reconcile to the actual payslip. Reconciliation can be time-consuming and can impact negatively on the delivery timeline. This scenario is common and the risk of it occurring should be addressed in the project planning process.

Parallel runs are common in the deployment of WFM and payroll solutions. Parallel runs are generally not seen in traditional methodologies but are sometimes seen in product supplier methodologies. There are two types of parallel: point-in-time parallel and actual parallel. Having previous experience when planning and executing either type of parallel run is invaluable in this area. Let's take a look at each of them.

Point-in-time parallel

These parallels are very common on payroll projects. They involve running payroll for a predetermined previous pay period and simulating that pay period's results in the new solution. While the description is straightforward, the permutations and nuances associated with planning and coordinating this are not.

If you are rolling out a new WFM and payroll solution at the same time, the challenges are further increased. There are often discretionary decisions made in the WFM system that influence pay results. If you don't know what led to this discretionary decision, there may be a reconciliation anomaly. Reconciliation anomalies usually have two main causes:

1. The site is paying differently to the EBA.
2. Discretionary decisions are being made, such as manual rounding, payment of overtime or variability in managers' application of rules.

Actual parallel

Actual parallels occur when you run the existing process (manual or automated) at the same time as the new automated process – that is, you have two systems of record for a defined period. This type of parallel can be useful when you want to bed in a new process and educate your team members in a pseudo-live environment and compare pay results in real time.

Many factors influence this type of testing, including the number of team members, ability to support the team members and ability to deal with configuration changes in a real-time environment.

CHANGE

'Change is quite possibly the single largest impact associated with any WFM project.'

Jarrod McGrath

As I have noted previously, WFM projects have people at their core. Delivery of business benefits requires process change and, subsequently, people change to achieve the outcome.

Using your people to drive change

Below are a number of roles I've seen utilised in organisations to help drive effective change. Don't get too hung up on the role titles; rather, focus on the key tasks each role is enacting.

Senior leadership

When senior leadership is proactively involved in the WFM project there is a better chance of achieving rapid success. It's important to make sure your leaders are at the right level and have the right mindset to drive change. For example, if you are part of a multifaceted organisation, and you are deploying the WFM solution over multiple business areas, the key leaders need to be at a level in the organisation where they have reach, influence and leverage over the different businesses. In this example, constant involvement and support from the CEO may be required.

Champions

The champions are your people who buy into the change and understand the benefits to the organisation, the people and the broader environment. The champions are generally operational managers within your organisation who have the strong respect of their teams. Champions must be able to canvass support and mitigate resistance and support the leaders and those at the coalface.

Your people

Your people are those at the coalface day-to-day; they adopt the new way of work as part of their daily routine. They use their mobile phone to see when a shift has been allocated, use a time-collection device to record hours worked and so on. Make sure they know what is in it for them.

EXPERT INSIGHT

Tracy Angwin – CEO at Australian Payroll Association – on change management

I'm observing that when employers are investing in payroll technology, they're not initially seeing the return on investment they expected. There's a reason for that, in my opinion, and that is that they haven't actually spent any time doing change management with their staff, or properly training their staff to use the new systems.

You can't just expect payroll managers and professionals to instinctively know what to do. These people care about what they do. They're judged by the mistakes they make, so if they find themselves with an extra 10 hours in the week due to process improvement they're going to use that time to check things. When you're using machine learning and AI, that's probably not a great use of their time; maybe they should be doing different types of checks.

It seems to me that not many organisations are providing any change management so that staff understand how their job might change. The investment is going into the technology, and it's fantastic – but very little investment is being put into the team to follow up; to ensure that the employer gets their return on investment.

In time, we're going to see payroll professionals doing much less operational work. When I first started in the payroll industry, a payroll officer would have a ruler and a couple of pens and it would all be done manually; then we got into Bundy Clocks and now we have AI. I think there will be a move from a more operational pay office to a more strategic, task-related pay office – one that will support the wider business. We should be doing much more valuable, strategic work in the pay office. We should be identifying the next staff members who are likely to leave based on the payroll data that we have. We should be analysing overtime and personal leave trends, based on location. We should be looking at leave liability issues and reporting that back to the employer.

I think it's slow, but that is the way that we're going in payroll. Employers need to realise that when they employ someone in payroll, they're not just looking for a data entry clerk or someone who understands numbers – the only way you're going to get a more proactive payroll function is to put well-trained, well-supported people in the seats. Don't expect that your pay office will change – no matter how much money you throw at technology – if you don't provide change management support.

Read the full transcript of my interview with Tracy at: smartwfm.com/book

Communications

The earlier in the process you can communicate why change is required, the lower the chance of guesswork happening in your organisation. I have found that the delivery of change messages is most effective if it comes from those who are part of your organisation and respected by your people.

Commencing a project with a meeting that involves everyone from senior leaders through to a representation of those at the coalface is beneficial. In this meeting, clearly indicate the business benefits and the key changes that will be coming. Have a transparent mechanism in place to solicit and communicate feedback regarding key items of concern.

Anna Santikos – Director of People, Culture and Learning at Montefiore – on internal communication

I can't emphasise internal consultation and communication enough – particularly with your staff who are at the coalface. It's just invaluable to get their insights around the needs, the things that are working well and the pain points. It's important to continue to consult with them as you progress.

For the implementation of our WFM system, we've established a working party that will continue to meet as we deploy the system. That working party consists of representatives from a range of different operational areas.

We've been very mindful in terms of how we communicate with our different stakeholders, making sure there's a very clear link to the strategy and a focus on consultation. When we roll out a new initiative that has come about as a result of staff feedback, we're very careful to make that link back. It's important staff know that you are hearing what they're saying, and that their feedback is actually driving care and service improvements, as well as improvements in terms of their experience and working environment.

Read the full transcript of my interview with Anna at: smartwfm.com/book

Business role changes

With the introduction of WFM you will almost certainly see adjusted or new roles within your organisation. Align job descriptions to this new way of working early. You may need to consider the introduction of new KPIs in order to align the organisational goals to your workforce. This may be necessary over a number of roles.

It may also be necessary to roll out and negotiate pay changes caused by EBA adjustments associated with the implementation.

A final note: even if everyone believes in the solution, if it is not usable it will not be adopted. Be careful not to lose sight of this in your implementation.

LEARNING

A common question I'm asked in regards to WFM projects is how and when people should be educated in the new way of work. While the answer to this will depend on your organisation's circumstances, there are a few considerations that may help with your decision.

The first four learning methods that are presented here are modern ways of conducting learning, while the latter three are more traditional in their approach.

Self-learning

As each day goes by, we are getting closer to training that is essentially self-learned – that is, the system is logical to a point that the team member can teach themselves. Take, for example, Facebook and Instagram, where new functions are added and people adapt to the changes naturally.

What we must take into consideration, however, is that the WFM business processes are unique to each individual organisation, and self-learning can present challenges for organisation-specific tasks. This is where self-learning can fall short.

Microlearning

Microlearning is a more realistic approach to supporting your people to learn in a WFM context. Microlearning breaks learning down into bite-size chunks. Taking this approach enables the leaning to be concentrated and more easy to complete, digest and retain. Courses can be developed and updated with a minimum of fuss. Platforms are becoming more commonly available to easily enable this, and are built with a mobile-first philosophy. The platforms work with push notifications, include gamification and make learning fun. I believe this type of learning will become the norm over the coming years.

Don't forget that as a valued reader, you and your team have free access to my new digital WFM online learning modules via the Smart WFM Academy. It might give you inspiration for developing a similar microlearning program for your organisation. Find it at: **smartwfm. com/book**.

In-product learning

Some product suppliers have moved to 'in-product' learning – where the learning paths and materials are built into the product. This has many advantages from a time, cost and acceptance perspective. Learning is available from the moment the product is turned on and can be updated and referenced in real time. The suppliers provide this learning and it remains current as new product releases are made available. This type of learning is particularly common in cloud environments.

While this learning supports the technology functionality it does not typically specifically reference your organisation or your specific business processes, unless you customise it.

Virtual reality learning

While I have not seen virtual reality (VR) learning used in WFM projects as yet I believe it will become prominent over the coming years. There are a number of technology suppliers developing cost-effective VR tools that are geared towards VR learning. Imagine, for example, seeing through VR how to execute the tasks that have been assigned to you for your current shift from the WFM task management software.

Short videos

These are generally short recordings lasting one or two minutes that demonstrate how to complete a specific task. Often they are taken in real time with a team member explaining how they use the technology.

Web recordings

Similar to short videos, but instead using a screen-flow capture tool, web recordings are used to demonstrate the system usage. Narratives can be added over the top of the recording to further enhance understanding.

Cheat sheets/quick reference guides

This method is still popular and tailored specifically to the task at hand. This output is generally a succinct one- or two-page overview.

DEPLOYMENT AND SUPPORT

WFM projects deal with your people, the way they get paid and your operating models. These are key considerations when you make any go-live decisions.

Deployment

Your options for deployment are typically phased or big-bang.

Phased

When you phase deployment, a section of your business is selected and it goes live at a given time. Take into consideration things such as support of legacy systems, pay periods, end of month, end of year, blackout periods, or other project/business initiatives.

It is difficult to separate rostering from EBA/pay results when going live, as rostering decisions have a direct impact on pay. For example, the times scheduled to start and stop work have a direct impact on the number of overtime hours. It's important to realise that your way of paying your employees and way of operating will change at the same time with the introduction of automated rostering and payment.

'Make sure you are truly ready
for the change. Don't bite
off more than you can chew,
and carefully consider which
business areas will go live at
the same time.'

—

Jarrod McGrath

Big-bang

A big-bang deployment is where all of your people, process and technology changes are adopted at the same time. Generally, big-bang deployments are the result of a compelling business need. For example, you may face significant contractual penalties for being on an existing system or you may be close to end-of-life for a legacy software solution.

My experiences of big-bang, especially at the large customer enterprise level, have not been positive, particularly for those at the coalface. Processes were not bedded down, payments were wrong, training was lacking, support structures were deficient. I am not saying don't adopt a big-bang go-live approach but, if you do, you need to have a high degree of diligence and governance in place to mitigate the risks associated with this method.

Staffing and support

WFM initiatives have a large footprint with your operational workforce. Consider your deployment and ongoing support structures well in advance to make sure you provide adequate support for your people. The larger the workforce, the more emphasis is required.

Consider how much staffing you will require to deploy and support your WFM solution. The change roles that were defined above can be retained throughout your deployment and support period. The answer to how much staffing you will require depends on the amount of business process and role changes that have been made.

Will you require staffing for each site? Many organisations also skill up their internal helpdesk (either with internal staff or consultants) to help everyone through this period.

Having daily meetings, sometimes known as stand-ups (onsite and/or remote) with your stakeholders and champions is valuable. Everybody gets to hear promptly what is working well and what is working not so well. Learning as a group can be powerful.

I challenge you to think through the implications of this and make sure you are ready for it. Consider the implications from a business operating model perspective and from a people payment (payroll) perspective. While these areas are complementary, they are quite different. The operating model impacts process and ways of working. Payments implicate what goes home in the pay packet each week. Both models take different skills and staffing to support.

Ongoing support

Once the project has concluded, who will support your WFM solutions in the future? You have the option to staff this internally, use external consultants, or a combination thereof.

The complexity in configuration with WFM solutions is often around the assessment and configuration of the business rules – in particular the award rules – along with integration components. Many large organisations pay careful consideration to upskilling or recruiting people with these skills. If the skills are used regularly and there is good variability in the role, this is a viable option. People with these skills will often lean towards working for the product supplier or consultancies due to the variety of work they get to perform.

Top take outs

- Understanding the current way of working will allow requirements and change to be understood, enabling adoption of the new systems.
- Sample artefacts are a great way to understand what is in place and how great the change will be.
- Taking ownership of your implementation process to achieve your outcomes is key.
- Supplier templates push responsibility on the organisation and don't always take into consideration changes to business process and workforce experience.

- Create an enterprise architecture to baseline your solution and to create delivery guidelines.

- Select a strong project team and set clear expectations about roles and responsibilities, and set KPIs.

- Clearly understand the business outcomes, scope and plan. Relay this to the project team regularly.

- Determine how the supplier methodology and traditional methodologies will be utilised.

- Utilise design thinking to ensure operating processes are designed with people and their experience first.

- Focus on modern learning approaches such as microlearning to engage and quickly educate your people.

- Create a flowing change, learning and support network.

Where to next?

We've now covered the Implement step, focusing on determining the steps necessary to complete a successful implementation. The next chapter looks at the tracking processes required to keep your implementation pointed in the right direction.

CHAPTER 8

TRACK

I have seen numerous governance methods applied across WFM initiatives. There are specific nuances with WFM initiatives, and if you have not experienced these before they can stymie the goal of achieving success. The approach to testing for correct pay results and determination of the best approach to deploy the solution are often hot topics and play an integral part in determining the success or failure of your initiative. Similarly, how to interpret an EBA seems straightforward, but once you scratch beneath the surface you can often discover some unexpected business interpretations. WFM implementations result in high-impact business change, which can lead to highly emotional outcomes for those involved. Having the right governance balance in place to drive business outcomes is of the utmost importance. This step in the 5-step workforce method will help you manage risk and ensure compliance.

HOW TO KEEP YOUR WFM INITIATIVE MOVING SUCCESSFULLY

The Track step (see figure 8.1) focuses on identification of the typical items I consider important to ensure success of your WFM initiative. The points I raise can be used as a checklist of WFM-related considerations. The topics discussed in this chapter and the other chapters in this book should be considered to complement your selected governance method. It may also be helpful to refer back to chapter 4.

Figure 8.1: Track

BENEFITS AND BUSINESS CASE

The benefits you are expecting your WFM implementation to bring to your organisation, which you outlined in your business case, should be supported by your project governance activities. They should be constantly reviewed and challenged as you move through the delivery program.

You should have locked down the benefits and business case at the outset of the WFM initiative and agreed on relevant items with all key stakeholders on the project, the implementation team and those people at the operational coalface. If you make the benefits and relevant areas from the business case visible, this will enable decisive decision-making throughout the project.

Understanding the benefits and business case is a foundation for success with your WFM initiative. It allows a link to be established between the benefits to the organisational and workforce goals. But it doesn't stop there – you need to continually track and review your progress towards it.

Over the years I have seen many organisations neglect to complete their business case, or forget to follow and adjust it as business needs change. COVID-19 is a perfect example of a situation causing business needs to change. Other examples are merger and acquisition activities, changing legislation, or different priorities as a result of new leadership. All of these events require you to check back in with your business case and adjust as necessary.

One way to ensure you are staying abreast of this is to utilise technology. Smart WFM's Apitome Software helps organisations rapidly deliver a business case in an agile and adaptive way. Find out more at: **smartwfm.com/apitome**.

THE PROJECT BOARD AND GOVERNANCE

The project board members play a key role in your WFM initiative as they keep it pointed in the right direction. I can't stress enough the importance of active participation in matters of governance by the project board members. Some of my key learnings in this regard follow.

Jason Averbook – CEO and Co-Founder at Leapgen – on governance

There's a word that people hate: 'governance'. And they hate it because they think it straps them down. But it's not strapping them down, it's keeping them aligned. It's like braces on your teeth, or training wheels on your bike. Governance protects you, and helps you stay in line; it doesn't stop you from being creative.

Read the full transcript of my interview with Jason at: smartwfm.com/book

Representation

As we have discussed already, WFM initiatives impact people. WFM projects cut across multiple areas of your business including operations, finance, payroll, IR and your suppliers. The representation of all the impacted business areas is important to achieve optimal results.

I am also a big believer in alternative points of view and transparency where possible. Having the relevant parties represented will ensure you are transparent, it will mean you benefit from a range of inputs and you will ultimately achieve a high-quality outcome. Having an independent, experienced member can also help; for example, a WFM delivery industry expert.

Subcommittees/working groups

You may want to include subcommittees or working groups to help clear the path for having some of your decisions accepted. In her expert insight in chapter 7, Anna Santikos – Director of People, Culture and Learning at Montefiore – spoke about the success her organisation has had as a result of setting up a regular working group.

Identify and set up your committees at the outset of your initiative. This will ensure you have the appropriate focus and representation available to work through key items. A common area for a subcommittee or working group is around EBA and rostering.

EBA

As identified in chapter 6, there are many things to consider associated with the EBA. These issues can be time-consuming and complex to work through. To recap, the key areas for consideration are:

- configuring directly from an EBA – payment to EBA or site practice – who makes the interpretation?
- different interpretations of the same EBA
- what to configure
- underpayment and overpayment.

Rostering

In chapter 6, I noted there are many things to consider associated with the operating models and rostering. These ways of working can be time-consuming and complex to work through. To recap, the key areas for consideration are:

- types of rostering
- labour standards
- roster optimisation
- centralised versus decentralised rostering.

Ensure the sub-committee has processes set up to monitor, inform and make decisions on each of these areas. Also check that there is support from IR and the unions where required.

METHODOLOGY

Your organisation, suppliers and delivery team will need to agree on a preferred methodology. Detailed discussion on methodology was provided in chapter 7. Your organisation may have its own implementation methodology, or you may use one of the traditional methodologies. In addition, your WFM supplier may have its own methodology built from years of delivery experience. Alignment and handover points with the methodologies will be required. For example, will your organisation's methodology reporting method be adopted, or will the supplier's be adopted?

This decision should be made at the outset of the WFM initiative, agreed by the governance committee and understood by all key stakeholders on the project and the implementation team. Making this clear at the outset of your initiative will ensure effective decision-making.

If you do not do this, you run a high risk of your suppliers pulling in different directions, or having differing views about the same topic or definition of an item of work. For example, people with a payroll background will often define a parallel run as comparing historical pay results for an agreed period. People with a WFM background will often define a parallel run as using your new WFM system for the current pay period as well as your legacy system.

Scope, plan and timeline

These are perhaps the most fundamental governance items. The scope, plan and timeline should be agreed by the governance committee. Ensure they are understood by all key stakeholders on the project, the implementation team and those people at the operational coalface too. Making this clear at the outset of your initiative will enable everyone to move in the same direction with clarity.

The governance committee and the PMs must be 100 per cent clear about this from the outset. If there is any uncertainty, address it as a priority. Document these areas in a way that everyone can understand. Anyone who is part of the WFM initiative should be able to explain the scope, plan and timeline of your WFM implementation (and they should give the same explanation).

Common questions that arise where these items can be thrown off track include:

- Which EBAs are in scope?
- Which rostering methods are in scope?

- Which sites are in scope?

- Which business areas are in scope?

- Which methodology will be used?

- What is the enterprise architecture?

- What is the testing process?

- What business process changes will be adopted?

- How many deployments will there be?

From a planning perspective, make it clear to your team members what they have to do, when they must do it and what your expectations are of their contribution.

Project risks and issues

Create a culture of acceptance and support around risks and issues. Provide a forum where your business, team and suppliers can raise these items without any fear of blame. Conduct regular reviews and address these items on their merit.

Change control

Change control is inevitable on WFM projects. The key areas where I see change are generally related to which EBAs are in scope, which rostering methods are in scope, which sites are in scope, which business areas are in scope, the number of deployments and your responsibilities versus your product supplier's responsibilities.

It is imperative that your delivery team understands the change control process. This is twofold. Firstly, it involves raising change items.

Secondly, once a change is agreed, you need to ensure that the outcome is communicated back to the team. It is easy for team members to avoid, not follow the process, or fail to adopt the change because they either do not understand it, or they don't know about it.

When considering change, check back to the benefits and business case to ensure the change is in alignment with the agreed organisational goals.

Project costs

Be realistic about your project costs and ensure that the management and governance team have the same understanding of the budget. Are you in alignment with your financial director; is your product supplier working from the same budget you are on?

If you require a cost adjustment, ensure the process for this is understood.

Reporting

Agree on your reporting standards at the outset of the WFM engagement. Consider what methodology or methodologies will be used to provide the reporting templates. Ensure the reporting formats and expectations are understood. Clearly communicate the frequency with which you require your reporting to be completed.

Be as transparent as possible in your project reporting. Keeping your teams informed – from senior leadership through to those at the coalface – is a key ingredient in keeping your WFM initiative on track.

Suppliers

It is common to have multiple suppliers working across a WFM initiative. Where relevant, introduce your suppliers to each other at the outset of the engagement to increase collaboration.

Suppliers generally work across multiple clients; make sure your priorities are understood by your suppliers and that they are applying the correct resources and focus to make your initiative successful.

Skill levels within the supplier's (and your own) teams will vary so ensure you are getting the appropriate skills for your investment. Sometimes suppliers will swap out staff due to competing priorities (as you will); this will place additional risk on the quality of delivery for your WFM initiative.

Understand at the start of your WFM initiative what value-add your supplier provides in areas such as account management, support, knowledge forums and so on. Keep your product and service suppliers accountable for their responsibilities.

Having a relationship in place with your supplier that separates the delivery and commercial negotiation can remove tensions that sometimes arise if the delivery person is having commercial discussions.

BUSINESS IMPACT

Before we leave the discussion on tracking your implementation, let's consider the business impact.

Business engagement, change and adoption

No matter how good your technical solution, the people in your business will determine the success or failure of your WFM initiative. If the people do not adopt the solution or don't have an optimal experience using it, the WFM initiative will not be successful.

Ensure you have representation across all your business areas and that you have a process in place to solicit objective feedback that feeds up to the governance level.

People assignment

In chapter 6 we looked at people requirements from a skills and timing perspective. Keep monitoring this throughout the course of the project. Not having the correct allocation of staff will lead to unnecessary stress and impede the quality of the solution. In some cases, I have seen this result in project team churn.

You need to answer two simple questions:

1. Are the people on the project happy?
2. Are the people in my business happy?

Top take outs

- The benefits you are expecting from your WFM implementation, which you outlined in your business case, should be supported by your project governance activities.

- Many WFM nuances are important to consider at a governance level to mitigate risk and increase organisational adoption.

- Set up subcommittees early in the engagement to deal with areas of high-impact business change. Common areas are EBA and rostering.

- Your business and its suppliers have substantial industry and product knowledge; their input to organisational governance is highly valuable.

- No matter how good your technical solution, the people in your business will determine the success or failure of your WFM initiative.

Where to next?

This chapter presented a number of ways to keep your WFM initiative on track. The next chapter focuses on measuring organisational value using the Smart WFM Maximum People Value (MPV) measurement framework.

CHAPTER 9

MEASURE

Traditionally we have measured organisational value in pure monetary terms. However, over the past few years – as I have managed my team at Smart WFM and consulted across large and small organisations all over the world – I have observed a shift in emphasis from shareholder return to broader stakeholder return. The range of stakeholders organisations are serving has increased dramatically to include their people (workforce), their families, the community and society at large. The World Economic Forum believes that for companies to continue to thrive, they 'need to build their resilience … through greater commitment to long-term, sustainable value creation that embraces the wider demands of people and planet.'[1] There is a greater concern about sustainability, diversity and inclusion and, more broadly, the organisation's expectations of the future.

---

1   World Economic Forum 2020, *Measuring Stakeholder Capitalism: Towards Common Metrics and Consistent Reporting of Sustainable Value Creation*, www3.weforum.org/docs/WEF_IBC_Measuring_Stakeholder_Capitalism_Report_2020.pdf.

'People – their passions, their trust, their experiences – and the organisation's contribution to society are driving organisational success and stakeholder return.'

—

Jarrod McGrath

This chapter presents a framework that can be used as guiding principles or applied as a measurement framework that balances and aligns people, technology and the environment to achieve the maximum people value. This in turn will provide the greatest organisation ROI, and overall stakeholder return.

This chapter has been totally rewritten since the first edition of this book and I believe this higher-level thinking and maturity will become the norm over coming years.

Tracking and measurement should be continuously completed at every stage of an implementation or business activity (see figure 9.1).

Figure 9.1: Measure

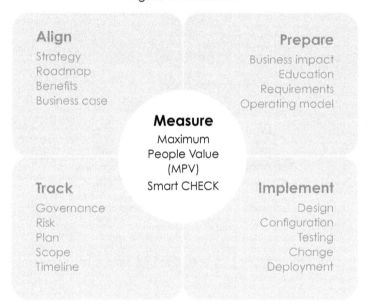

MEASURING AND MAXIMISING PEOPLE VALUE

At the heart of tracking and measurement is the concept that value is not just about financial dollars and profit – rather, value exists in multiple forms within your organisation. Ultimately, we all want to achieve and maximise the people value in our business. If we achieve that, the other forms of value – such as financial, shareholder, and societal – will also be achieved. In other words, a focus on your people value is not mutually exclusive to other forms of value.

The Smart WFM Maximum People Value (MPV) measurement framework shown in figure 9.2 is a comprehensive framework to support tracking and measurement.

Figure 9.2: Maximum People Value (MPV) measurement framework

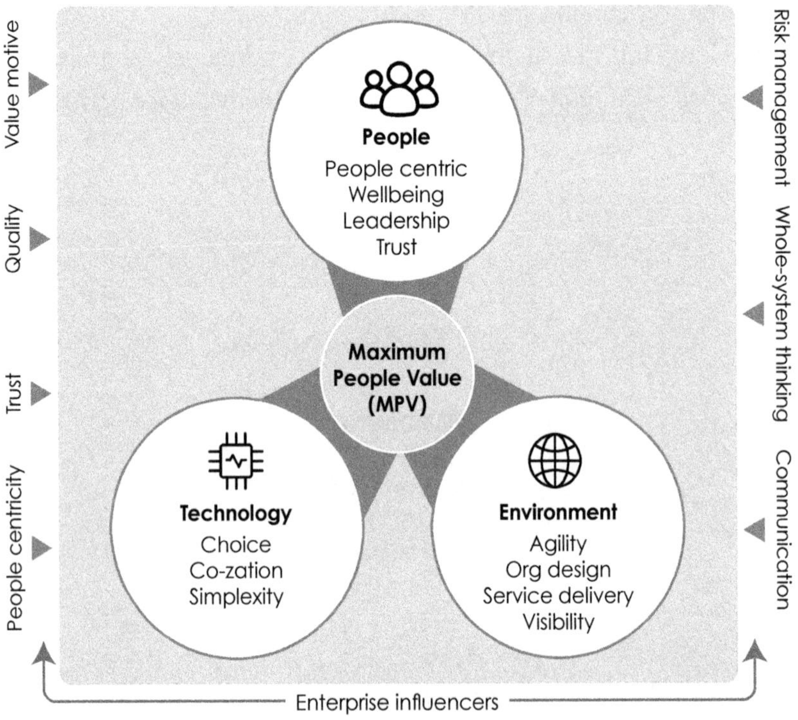

Three Focal Points

The inner core of the framework comprises three Focal Points:

1. People
2. Technology
3. Environment.

Everything we do in a digital workplace will always have these three components as part of the design.

In the past, these three Focal Points were often owned and managed in isolated ways, which gave rise to power struggles, a siloed mentality and less-than-optimal outcomes.

If you want to maximise people value, it's imperative that these three Focal Points are in complete alignment and that this is accepted by all owners and contributors. A single Focal Point cannot operate optimally unless the other two are given equal consideration.

A critical aspect of this model is that the three Focal Points impact each other in a bidirectional manner. In the past, for example, the IT function may have provided a piece of software to Operations or Finance, with the understanding that the receiving department took functional ownership of the software, and IT would maintain the technology. This is an example of a one-way relationship. In a digital workforce, this is no longer an appropriate response, as we are in a continuous state of flux.

Let's take an example of wellbeing in your organisation. The decisions you make to configure a piece of software have an impact on an employee's wellbeing. For example, your WFM solution may raise a flag around fatigue to the employee and line manager when excessive hours are worked – this is represented in the framework as the 'Technology' to 'People' direction. But the state of an employee's wellbeing at any point in time should also be able to influence the technology. This is the 'People' to 'Technology' direction. For example, let's say the fatigued employee uses the mobile app on her way home to set her status to 'not available' for the next day – the technology will accept the new input and find a replacement worker. Choice is an example of a key principle in modern technology design, and this example shows how it can offer flexibility to support a human behavioural response. In this situation it has helped manage fatigue, but also subconsciously acknowledges your organisation's commitment to the value of people.

Ongoing monitoring and measurement will provide excellent insights into continuous improvement, ensuring you keep your people value at the maximum possible level.

Of the three Focal Points, People and Technology will probably be the most familiar to you. The People Focal Point is typically the starting point for all people matters. This is not confined to a functional activity such as those run by the HR department; it's broader than that. For example, it is the starting point for a strategic direction around people, such as people-centricity, or it could be a cultural launchpad to focus on trust.

Likewise, the Technology Focal Point should not be equated to the IT function. While it will house these activities, concepts such as *choice* – the ability for technology to provide or restrict this based on human response – would fall into this Focal Point. 'Co-zation' – the understanding that standardisation and personalisation are not polar opposites, but can be achieved in unison – also falls under technology. Our previous example of how fatigue was managed shows that personalisation did not undermine the overall process. 'Simplexity' – an understanding that a symbiotic relationship exists between simplicity and complexity – is an important underlying concept to deploying technology that improves people value.

The Environment Focal Point is probably less recognised in this context. We all create many varied environments in our organisational structures. When COVID-19 hit, we quickly created work-from-home environments. Our company culture is an environment, as are your virtual reality learning offerings and your community support program. Anything that creates a set of rules to define a physical or virtual space, a mission, a corporate philosophy (such as 'Protecting our Planet') or a location can be considered an environment.

With this in mind, you can easily see that by adding people and technology bidirectional links to an environment requires a lot of thought to ensure we can maximise value and experience. COVID-19 gave us a unique opportunity to see this play out globally. Consider how trust and working from home played out in your organisation. Did tools such as Zoom and Teams improve or worsen people's well-being? Did your work-from-home environment clash with or support your onsite environment?

Enterprise Influencers

The Maximum People Value (MPV) measurement framework includes seven Enterprise Influencers:

1. Value motive
2. Quality
3. Trust
4. People centricity
5. Risk management
6. Whole-system thinking
7. Communication.

These Enterprise Influencers provide an important reality check, giving you a snapshot of how you are currently operating. By measuring these Enterprise Influencers, you will have a greater appreciation of your ability to maximise people value in any project or business activity undertaken.

Table 9.1 provides more information about each of the Enterprise Influencers.

Table 9.1: The seven Enterprise Influencers

Enterprise Influencer	Explanation
Value motive	This influencer is a measure that determines whether your organisation places emphasis on one form of value to the detriment of others. For example, if your organisation places financial success and profit above all else, that will drive particular behaviours within your organisation – often at the expense of other types of value such as people, community, planet, stakeholder, product, service or capital.
Quality	The extent to which quality programs and continuous improvement philosophies exist in the minds of all employees.

Enterprise Influencer	Explanation
Trust	The level of trust and cooperation that exists between all people in the organisation, as well as between the organisation and external groups such as the supply chain, community and broader society.
People centricity	The extent to which the organisation prioritises human capability and expectations.
Risk management	The extent to which people risk is managed across the organisation.
Whole-system thinking	The level of integration between strategic plans and organisational design.
Communication	The degree of openness, honesty and transparency in communication practices internally as well as externally to suppliers, clients, customers, community and society.

Enterprise Influencers moderate the maximum value you are able to attain. For example, if communication is an excellent attribute of your organisation, then you are likely to find immediate value by introducing Microsoft Teams as your collaboration platform.

Let's consider a simple example of implementing a new SaaS payroll system which has some compelling end-user features. If, however, there are employee concerns about how awards (payment rules) are being interpreted at your company, the overall level of trust in your payroll capability may be low. The question is, how will that low level of trust influence your payroll system implementation and the achievement of MPV? How could you adjust your program of work to mitigate some of that influence? The reality is that you may not be able to significantly change the level of trust in your organisation in the short term, but by measuring it and understanding its implications you can make necessary project adjustments to compensate.

EXPERT INSIGHT

Tracy Angwin – CEO at Australian Payroll Association – on trust in payroll capability

When a leader presents a transformation project to employees, the first question she will invariably be asked is, 'When are you going to figure out how to pay us correctly?' If your payroll function is not a part of the organisation that is trusted, this will undermine your entire transformation project. You'll have to fix that before you can even think about rolling out your transformation strategy.

Read the full transcript of my interview with Tracy at: smartwfm.com/book

In some cases your project may become a catalyst to improve the overall levels of trust, communication or risk management in your organisation – these opportunities can be exceptionally valuable to the overall achievement of MPV.

The higher the seven Enterprise Influencers score individually and collectively, the greater the opportunity is to maximise your people value. The converse is also true – the lower your score, the less likely your people (and other) values will achieve their planned objectives.

By measuring the outer Enterprise Influencers, as well as the bidirectional relationships between the three Focal Points, you will be able to determine an MPV score. This becomes an initial baseline from which you can aim to continually improve – whether by creating improvement at the enterprise level, operational level or project level. Measurement provides a great way to determine your priorities, as well as triggering important discussions with stakeholders about creating and improving value in your organisation.

I believe this holistic mindset and approach to measuring value will become mainstream and mature significantly over the next few years.

Find out more about the MPV framework at **smartwfm.com/book**.

Smart CHECK

You will recall I introduced Smart CHECK when I defined the 5-step workforce method in chapter 4. At any time during the business life-cycle, a Smart CHECK can be completed to measure where you are at and provide recommendations on what you need to do next. The Smart WFM team can provide your organisation with a personalised Smart CHECK framework.

Top take outs

- At the heart of tracking and measurement is the concept that value exists in multiple forms within your organisation beyond pure monetary value.
- Use a higher-level thinking framework, such as the Smart WFM Maximum People Value (MPV) measurement framework, to continually measure your business outcomes.
- The Focal Points for measurement balance people, technology and environment.
- The seven Enterprise Influencers enable you to moderate how you are currently operating.
- Use a Smart CHECK at any time during your initiative to mark where you are at and what you need to do next.

Where to next?

This chapter provided an overview of the steps to ensure the business benefits of your organisation's WFM initiative are met.

In the next chapter, we'll pull together key themes that are essential for anyone undertaking digital transformation to grasp.

CHAPTER 10

THE DIGITAL WORKFORCE OF TODAY AND THE FUTURE

With the second edition of *The Digital Workforce* I realised the importance of including a chapter looking towards the future. After I completed the expert interviews for this edition, along with my own learnings, I could see key themes emerging that would help organisations drive success today and in the future.

One of the questions I asked my interviewees was, 'What does the digital workforce of the future look like?' The consistent answer was that our actions of today provide the pathway to the future. Digital technology has traditionally had low uptake because of poor functionality or poor people experience, but over the last couple of years these barriers have been removed due to rapid technological advancements and mindset shifts. The COVID-19 pandemic also forced many reluctant organisations to take the plunge into digital workforce management

'People are more important than ever. We will maximise their value when we unleash their potential coupled with building a collaboration between algorithms and machines. This is the path to obtain maximum organisational and stakeholder value.'

—

Jarrod McGrath

before they perhaps felt ready. All of this has made it even more critical that organisations and WFM experts learn from each other and put steps in place to ensure their workplaces are not left behind.

Here are some of the key themes that are essential for anyone undertaking digital transformation to grasp and absorb. They are a baseline for achieving maximum people value and achieving the greatest organisational value and stakeholder return.

PEOPLE ARE THE EPICENTRE OF EVERYTHING WE DO

Everything I see and everyone I speak to makes it clearer and clearer that people are at the epicentre of a successful digital future.

Skills are changing but overall the evidence indicates that there will be more jobs into the future then there are now. The new world of work brings together people, algorithms and machines. Let's revisit our diagram from chapter 3 (see figure 10.1).

Figure 10.1: The digital workforce

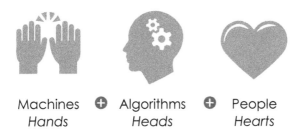

| Machines | ➕ | Algorithms | ➕ | People |
| *Hands* | | *Heads* | | *Hearts* |

When you think about it like this, it really breaks this changing work environment down to something that is easy to understand.

I recently had the pleasure of speaking with a prominent MP, who said there was a sense of trepidation and fear among his constituents about machines and technology, and what this means for people in the future of work. I hope that the insights and evidence from this book help dispel that fear.

It's how we combine the power of people and technology into a single, seamless capability that will make the difference. Once we stop viewing technology as a tool and see it as a collaborator, our understanding of progress will be altered forever and we will see that the future is full of opportunities, not threats.

WELLBEING TAKES ON NEW MEANING

The global pandemic taught us that rapid change requires rapid realisation of the impact. Wellbeing is not a short-term goal, as the impact of change takes time to manifest. The question is how we deal with wellbeing when we are thrust into an unknown situation.

In my experience I have observed that we often think of wellbeing in a very narrow sense, without realising the opportunity we have with technology and the environments we create to improve wellbeing in the broadest sense: physical, mental, social, financial, intellectual and emotional.

'Wellbeing is now mainstream and must be a key part of your workforce strategy.'

Jarrod McGrath

EXPERT INSIGHT

Georgegina Poulos – Global Director People T2 and Global Retail Operations at Unilever – on wellbeing

The role of people will always be number one – we can't get away from that. You can't have a thriving business without great people. I think the focus on mental health, wellbeing, the real self, the whole self, will continue into the future.

As you become more digital, it's also harder to turn off. We need to have really clear boundaries around this. If you have any device, anytime, anywhere, you need to build in practices to give yourself time to relax and switch off. I think that's a real barrier not just for us as an organisation, but in society.

The office was a place to go to work; its four walls provided a physical space entirely devoted to work. Now, the home has become the gym, the office, the movie theatre, the kids' playground, the hospital, the kitchen, the restaurant, you name it. I think what we really need to focus on now is redefining the boundaries of the home and work within this flexible environment, and figuring out how they come together to support wellbeing as well as business success.

Read the full transcripts of my interviews with Georgegina at: smartwfm.com/book

LEADERSHIP NEEDS TRANSFORMING, TOO

Digital transformation cannot take place without a change in the way leadership happens in your organisation. The COVID-19 pandemic was a good example of how the need to trust changed the way we led. I observed many leaders having difficulty letting go of the 'I need to see you to know you are productive' leadership style. This ties into the future culture change. Leaders must learn to become more compassionate and realise that there are many different approaches to achieving agreed outcomes – without losing professionalism.

> 'True digital transformation and the alignment of people, algorithms and machines requires a new way of thinking.'

Jarrod McGrath

AGILITY ISN'T OPTIONAL

COVID-19 proved to the world the importance of agility. Working from home is perhaps the best example of this. Compared to the beginning of 2020, most organisations' positions on working from home have significantly changed. This pivot was required in many cases for organisations to remain commercially viable by allowing them to operate while people were required to stay at home.

It's more important than ever for organisations to have a digital strategy that is completely aligned to business drivers. If business drivers or focus changes, the strategy and its roadmap for delivery need to change at the drop of a dime.

The organisation business drivers, digital strategy and roadmap need to clearly define the benefits and measures that will be achieved from the actions taken. Rapid changes need to be communicated quickly and efficiently from the coalface, senior leadership, other stakeholders and sometimes governments alike.

Agile skills development is also necessary to support instantaneous changes in business drivers and the rapid uptake of digital technology.

> '**Agile business models are required to support changing business drivers, allowing organisations to meet people expectations and remain commercially viable.**'
>
> **Jarrod McGrath**

PEOPLE EXPERIENCE IS EVERYTHING

When enterprise resource planning (ERP) became popular in the late '90s there was an expectation that you had to adopt technology regardless of the human experience, as the optimal process was often limited by the technology.

Today, technology has evolved to a point where organisations are not limited in their ability to drive a superior people experience. People processes are now often designed taking a human-centered 'design thinking' approach, where the 'persona' of the employee or customer is a central tool in delivering a superior people and process experience underpinned by technology.

We are seeing a massive investment in people experience today, and this will continue. We'll see a closer relationship between the customer and the employee with ubiquitous collaboration, and data will be knitted together in a seamless way. All interactions both inside and outside the organisation will be 'remembered' and 'served up' instantaneously.

EXPERT INSIGHT

Jason Averbook – CEO and Co-Founder at Leapgen – on customer experience

We need to think about how we bring staff and customers together – because for the most part, we're living on separate islands. I do my work on my island, and who do I communicate with? The people on my island.

If I want to communicate with another island, which is my customer, what do I have to do? Chances are I'm not on their network, so I can't communicate with them via Slack or an instant message. Instead, I have to send them an email. Hopefully, it gets through their filters. Hopefully, they read it. Perhaps they might respond to it. And then, maybe they'll send the telegram back across the ocean, into my email on my island.

That's too slow. That speed isn't acceptable. How do I get things done inside my organisation? I'm Slacking with people. I'm Teamsing with people. I'm getting answers quickly. How do I get something done with a customer? I use email, phone calls and voicemail. In other words, we've figured out how to accelerate communication within our organisations, but communicating with our customers still relies on ancient methods.

'People expect a great experience – whether that be as a customer or an employee. We will continue to see increased focus to integrate people, processes and technology with human-centered design at the core.'

Jarrod McGrath

There has been a lot of hype recently about Salesforce's acquisition of Slack. To me, it's not so much about Slack and Salesforce as it is about bringing customers and organisations into one, so we can communicate with customers using the same modern methods we use to communicate within our teams.

Read the full transcript of my interview with Jason at: smartwfm.com/book

TRANSPARENCY AND TRUST WILL MAKE OR BREAK PEOPLE ORGANISATIONS

Trust, in my view, is a word that has been overused in recent times. I have seen examples of people and organisations using this term purely as a sales tool to enable an outcome. Once the sale is made or the trust is given there is often a misalignment of expectation when it comes to delivering on the promise.

Trust is also relative. For example, you might trust an organisation to pay your salary but not trust them to pay you correctly, because they have been called out for underpayment in the past and did not transparently let staff know about it.

Trust must also extend to diversity and inclusion – its not about just inviting someone to the party, but actually including their dance in the organisational culture.

There is also a new type of trust we need to explore: that of our trust in technology. As the prevalence of AI grows we actually run greater risk of creating mistrust, unless we deal with the ethics of technology in the workplace.

'Everyone should receive transparent information that enables trust to be earnt. We also need to consider trust in relation to AI.'

Jarrod McGrath

Georgegina Poulos – Global Director People T2 and Global Retail Operations at Unilever – on inclusion

The future is all about celebrating difference to make a difference, and having an inclusive environment. When we think about the digital landscape, we need to make sure it's inclusive, it's accessible and we're not leaving anyone behind. When we're designing solutions, whether it's in the physical workplace or in the virtual workplace, we must think of everybody.

There's never been a bigger impact on social justice than the global pandemic. We, as corporate citizens, all have a role to play. I'm super proud that T2 has inclusion and social justice firmly on its agenda. We are dedicated to welcoming all cultures, all ages, all religions and all lifestyles. It's an exciting future, I think.

Read the full transcripts of my interviews with Georgegina at: smartwfm.com/book

THE WORKFORCE DEMANDS A COMPLETE VIEW OF ITS IMPACT ON WORLD LONGEVITY

Once upon a time, an organisation's view of its workers was very much authoritarian: 'I pay you, you work for me and I tell you what to do.' Can you imagine if this was still the case?

Today, organisations recognise that their people are their lifeblood. The next step is to recognise that people's value extends far beyond work. People are starting to question the impact the organisation's actions have on their family and friends, the economy, the environment, the planet and the longevity of humankind.

'Future proofed workplaces will focus on sustainable practices while being mindful of the impacts on all stakeholders.'

Jarrod McGrath

Georgegina Poulos – Global Director People T2 and Global Retail Operations at Unilever – on sustainability

In 2010, Unilever set out on a journey to become the world's most sustainable business. We wanted to prove that growth doesn't have to come at the expense of people and planet; to show that business can be a force for good.

We are super proud at T2 to be a Certified B Corporation – we got our accreditation in 2020. A Certified B Corporation is a business that balances purpose and profit. So, that means that we have been independently assessed to meet a level of criteria around sustainability, diversity and inclusion, ethical work practices and so on.

In order to get and maintain that accreditation, we actually have to live our purpose and be sustainable. Sustainability is one of our three core pillars: people, product, planet. So, whether it's reducing paper through digital processes, looking at our footprint and offsetting it, recycling, reusing, recompressing, composting – we've done some amazing work.

Being sustainable has an impact on attracting and retaining team members as well as customers. Our team members have really embraced our purpose; we recently did an engagement survey and the top three factors to receive 90-plus percentage scores were connecting to our values; understanding our values; and that our purpose is right for our business.

We've done a lot of work on that in the last six to eight months. We've run a values campaign where team members have shared with us how they bring our values to life. And it's paid off. People are really connected to it and believe it's important, and are holding us accountable.

Read the full transcripts of my interviews with Georgegina at: smartwfm.com/book

EXPERT INSIGHT

Aron Ain – CEO of UKG (Ultimate Kronos Group) – on driving the greater good

I think people want to work for a place that makes a difference – not just inside the company walls, but also in the broader community.

Their own expectations are they want to make a difference in their communities and the world. Social tools make that much easier to do. It's impacting philanthropy, it's impacting volunteerism, it's impacting how people spend their time.

At our company, we have a GiveInspired program, which supports the community. And it's not just that; it's beyond just giving. It's also facilitating volunteering and encouraging that to happen. I know it makes us an attractive employer.

People join companies because of the company. They also decide to stay at the company because of the experience they have while they're there. You have to work in both dimensions around your brand.

Read the full transcripts of my interviews with Aron at: smartwfm.com/book

THE CHANGING ROLE OF THE ORGANISATION

As I mentioned in the preface, when I wrote the first edition of this book I had recently read *The Fourth Industrial Revolution* by Klaus Schwab, Founder and Executive Chairman of the World Economic

Forum. Klaus voiced his concern that governments and policymakers may not be able to keep up with the pace of change brought about by digital disruption. Enter COVID-19, and the pace of change accelerated to a whole new level.

Since the global pandemic, organisations have had to take greater responsibility for the wellbeing and mental health of their staff. People's homes became workplaces and education centres, as well as being places for relaxation. Overnight, organisations needed to take responsibility for helping their people strike a balance across these areas; wellbeing became critical to commercial longevity.

EXPERT INSIGHT

Georgegina Poulos – Global Director People T2 and Global Retail Operations at Unilever – on the post-COVID workplace

COVID-19 has obviously been a huge challenge for organisations across the globe. I've been working with the global incident management team on setting very clear protocols – we have our own tier system within Unilever, T2 and the other businesses within the family. In some cases, our protocols are more stringent than the government's; in other cases, we follow government, but it's not as simple as, 'Now the government says we can do this, so we will'.

It's been a real journey. If you think about it, late 2019 we experienced one of the worst bushfires that we've ever encountered in Australian history. Then we had floods, and then we went back to bushfires, and then we moved into a pandemic. So, we have really been in crisis management or incident management since November 2019. How do we prepare our teams for this ever-changing environment?

We were one of the first organisations to mobilise our teams to get them home. Early in March 2020, we moved everybody in our Melbourne and UK offices to work from home. We had around 130 to 140 people all set up at home with Teams and mobile devices within 24 hours – thinking we would be working from home for about four weeks.

We really thought about our essential workers – if we use the language of the pandemic around who needed to come into the office and couldn't really work from home – as our most vulnerable team members, but others were struggling, too. Domestic violence was increasing; there was depression, isolation, a whole range of things. So, we ran surveys throughout the period to check in with our teams. We kept our office open for two days per week under really strict protocols for about five people.

One of the reasons we wanted to get people home was for their safety, but it also freed up infrastructure. It allowed those who needed to move around to do so more safely. But now, just as we want the economy to be rebuilt for our business, we also need to contribute to our own communities. We want people to come back in to the office to support the area that we work in, but also to create that sense of belonging and connection.

The role of the office is now really different. When it comes to the everyday, high-focus work, well, you can do that at home. But when we need to be innovative and collaborative, to bring people together, that's when the office comes into play. It's a catalyst for that type of thinking. And that's why we need to encourage people to come back.

We did a survey and found that about 70 per cent of our team members would like to work two to three days from home, and the rest of the time in the office. And that's, on average, similar to global data. So the challenge now is how do we think about the workplace in a different way? Because it'll be a hybrid working environment. There'll be people on the phone, there'll be people in the room, there'll be people on the screen. How do you keep everybody engaged? And what new culture is required for this type of working environment?

'If I can't see you, I can't lead you' is a common myth. But leading teams virtually is still leading teams. It's based on

'CEOs and senior leaders will have more responsibility for people than ever before. We will see a rapid increase in the importance of the organisation to people's lives, both inside and outside the workplace.'

Jarrod McGrath

the same principles: you set your expectations, you have your catch-ups and you talk about performance.

The beauty of the post-COVID workplace is that nine to five is no longer a given. We now need to think more broadly. What is the span of hours where people are most productive? I'm a super-early person. I don't expect my team to be on calls at 6 am when I'm up, but it works for me because it frees up my time. It doesn't really matter what time the results are being delivered, as long as they are being delivered, and the customers' needs are being met.

Read the full transcripts of my interviews with Georgegina at: smartwfm.com/book

EXPERT INSIGHT

Aron Ain – CEO of UKG (Ultimate Kronos Group) – on the changing role of the organisation

The COVID-19 pandemic emphasised that we must put people first. Organisations and leaders must rise to the occasion when things are bad. Being in a situation like a global pandemic and having to figure out how to look after the needs of all the people who work for us – this represents a remarkable responsibility.

I wake up every morning thinking about what I am going to do today to look after the needs of the 12,800 people who work for us, and their families. I go to bed every night and I reflect on how I did that day looking after those people's needs. It's my number one priority. It's not my *only* priority, but it's my number one priority.

I think the elected officials and other leaders that citizens normally look to for comfort and guidance are not doing an effective job in many parts of the world. So I think it falls on the shoulders of organisations, CEOs in particular, to step up to the plate and extend leadership and values more than ever.

My role is to provide direction and comfort to people, and I take that responsibility really seriously because it's needed now more than ever.

We have great people working for us today. We have to keep working hard to retain them, by creating an environment where people want to stay in our company. We have to create an environment where our people can excel, by giving them the right managers and the tools to do their job, and communicating with them and trusting them and being transparent and taking care of them.

Organisations must grasp that our people are remarkable assets that help us be better in every way. Those are the organisations that will successfully serve their customers and the people who work for them.

Read the full transcripts of my interviews with Aron at: smartwfm.com/book

THE CHANGING ROLE OF HR

I am sure many of you would relate to comments like, 'It's not in my job remit,' or, 'That is the responsibility of another department'. Far too often we hear comments like this and it stifles business collaboration, innovation and growth. If we are truly going to create a working environment that achieves the maximum people value we need to change our mindset and think more holistically.

EXPERT INSIGHT

Jason Averbook – CEO and Co-Founder at Leapgen – on the changing role of HR

I believe HR is going to shift from focusing on compliance to focusing on how we ensure that humans bring their best selves to work. So, instead of checking up on people, HR will be checking in on people. Instead of monitoring people, they'll be enabling people.

This means not asking team members once a year how they're feeling, but asking them that every day. Our HR representative is going to be like a coach, rather than someone we regret talking to.

I also believe that, as long as HR organisations have diversity and inclusion functions that are separate from our business processes, everything is going to be seen as separate. Instead, we need to think about the whole person in a holistic way. And that means we have to change the way HR thinks.

Diversity and inclusion should be infused into everything we do on a daily basis; it shouldn't be a once a year activity where we check for quotas and be done. That's where we've done a massive disservice to this whole concept.

So, how does the HR organisation shift from counting heads to making heads count? I can't just count people. If I'm in a business of counting people, I'm not in HR. There's no human in that.

HR is about humanity. The way that I think about it is as three different body parts: hands, heads, and hearts. And this is going to be really important for every HR organisation around the world to think about: machines are really good at *hands* work. In fact, machines are *better* at hands work than people are. We're not good at it. We make errors. We 'fat finger' stuff all the time.

But what people are great at is *hearts* work. People are great at taking data and being able to use that data to tell stories, and to make decisions. That's *heads* work.

Linking this back to diversity and inclusion: we can't just let a bot choose who we hire and be done with it. We need heart and head tied to that decision. So, the way that we have to think about the HR function into the future is, how do we automate as much as we can of the hands work, so that we can leverage our human resources for the heads work and the hearts work?

If we can do that, and create those journeys, then we're going to be focused on the right things around the humanity part of human resources, instead of the counting humans part of human resources.

We have to intentionally make space for this. We just don't naturally have time to let our intuition speak. If we're too busy checking boxes, or collecting forms, or entering data, we don't have time for the head or heart work. And what happens? It just doesn't happen. We have to be intentional about creating the space to let intuition come into play.

Read the full transcript of my interview with Jason at: smartwfm.com/book

HR has become more important then ever in business. As Jason Averbook says, HR needs to move from counting heads to making heads count. With digital transformation (accelerated by COVID-19), people will need to learn how to work alongside algorithms and machines. People should be at the core of business strategy from the coalface through to senior leadership across all business functions both inside and outside the workplace.

EXPERT INSIGHT

Anna Santikos – Director of People, Culture and Learning at Montefiore – on the changing role of HR

Since I embarked on my career, there's been enormous change around the HR function and its role in organisations. During my time at Montefiore there has been significant changes in the composition of the team and the design of roles within it. I think we've seen that reflected in the titling of the function. At Montefiore, we retitled HR several years ago – we're now People and Culture.

When I began my career, the HR function was quite transactional, administrative, very much focused on aspects like making sure that personnel records were maintained and that the organisation was compliant in terms of wages and benefits – which, of course, still needs to be done today.

There seems to be a growing recognition of the importance of the HR team – however, it's now described in terms of supporting the organisation to achieve its objectives. It's more of a partnering approach across the different areas of an organisation and we have an advisory role. We look at how we can enhance workforce capability. We're focused more on the people strategy rather than the transactional and administrative side.

Technology has been key to affecting that change. Through different platforms we've been able to achieve great efficiencies around our record-keeping, how we recruit and all of the administration associated with recruitment onboarding.

HR also now has a part to play in making sure managers have the skills required to support the organisational objectives via the operational people functions.

Read the full transcript of my interview with Anna at: smartwfm.com/book

In the first edition of *The Digital Workforce* I predicted that WFM and HR would combine to provide a complete people picture, as depicted in figure 10.2.

This symbiosis between WFM and HR is perhaps even more critical than ever today. It exemplifies that the whole is greater than the sum of parts. WFM provides the tools for workers at the coalface to do their day-to-day work (for example, communications tools, schedules, availability, requesting leave); it also allows staff to engage more deeply with their managers about their work and life, both inside and outside the organisation. Without these broader considerations, any strategy related to people is incomplete.

Today I would represent the symbiosis between WFM and HR as per figure 10.3.

Figure 10.2: The complete people picture

WFM impacts in your business

- Payroll
- Staff
- Supervisors
- IT
- Finance
- Operations management
- HR
- Senior management
- Workforce robots

WFM + HR

- ↑ Efficient processes
- ↑ Financial understanding
- ↑ Complete view of workforce
- ↑ Culture
- ↑ Personalisation
- ↑ Brand loyalty
- ↑ Inspiration
- ↑ Purpose
- ↑ Automation
- ↑ Efficiency
- ↑ Value add
- ↑ Mobility
- ↑ Dispersed workforce

Your complete people picture

Figure 10.3: The symbiosis between WFM and HR

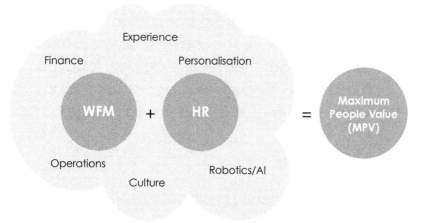

Experience

Finance

Personalisation

WFM + **HR** = **Maximum People Value (MPV)**

Operations

Culture

Robotics/AI

'COVID-19 taught business the importance of people. The opportunity for HR to elevate people value has never been greater'.

Jarrod McGrath

SERVICE DELIVERY IS REDEFINED

I have mentioned several times in this book that organisations need to take responsibility for their own destiny. Product vendors focus on technology, but not necessarily business outcomes or people and process transformation.

For traditional service organisations that consult and focus on transformation, most of their existing commercial models are profit-and-loss driven and work in a siloed nature across their departments (technology, advisory, implementation, change and so on).

My observation is that there are few people who are well equipped with the right skills to accurately consult on today's organisation, and what its people need to be effective and most valuable.

'Don't just assume that traditional consultancies are skilled and ready to support your organisation. Ensure they have invested in their people, and that their service delivery function is structured to support your success and your business outcomes in a modern digital age.'

Jarrod McGrath

I see more and more that organisations are looking for coaching or 'white glove' services as and when they need them to assist their internal teams with the knowledge required to transition or transform their organisation efficiently and effectively. The key is to choose your service delivery organisation carefully, ensuring they are aligned with your business requirements and people and process strategy before bringing them on board.

***

While the future no doubt holds challenges for us all, I truly believe we should all feel excited and positive about the opportunities available. We have all the people, processes and technology available to support any organisation's workforce evolution – inside the workplace and beyond.

It's time for leaders to take responsibility for their organisation's destiny. It is up to us to capitalise on the opportunities available to us, and continue to raise the bar – with people, of course, being at the centre of everything that we do.

Top take outs

- People are at the epicentre of everything we do.
- Digital transformation cannot take place without trust from the coalface across all the stakeholders inside and outside your organisation.
- Agile skills development is also necessary to support instantaneous changes in business drivers and the rapid uptake of digital technology.
- HR needs to move from counting heads to making heads count.
- Organisations need to take responsibility for their own destiny.

Where to next?

The next step is for you to put the learnings and experiences from this book into practice. I wish you luck with your people-based WFM initiatives.

CONCLUSION

I hope this book has succeeded in achieving some of the objectives I had when I decided to update it, which as you may recall were:

1. To examine WFM through a business-focused lens, using real-life examples and expert opinions

2. To provide leaders and organisations with the intelligence required to predict and conquer key workforce-related issues

3. To help organisations maximise the value of their people, and ultimately overall organisation value, by building awareness of and leveraging the triggers that create people value

4. To present my proven 5-step workforce method, which can help any organisation deliver effective workforce management and value.

It's up to you now to take these learnings and apply them in ways that make sense to achieve your organisation's WFM outcome. As our knowledge grows, our ability to manage our workforce more effectively will also grow.

I trust that as we network in this digital age and continue to learn, the business, employee, customer and social outcomes continue to become greater.

I'll leave you with a quote from Walt Disney, which I feel resonates even more strongly in this second edition of *The Digital Workforce*:

'Our greatest natural resource is the minds of our children.'

ACKNOWLEDGMENTS

There are many friends, partners and colleagues around me who I have learned from; they have supported the ideas you find in this book and put trust in me to write it. Thank you to everyone for enabling this to happen. I can't put into words how personally satisfying it was to write this second edition of my book; I feel blessed and privileged to have written it for you.

As part of my ongoing education and desire to learn, I read countless books, blogs and articles; watch videos; listen to podcasts; and personally consult as many experts as I can find to talk to.

A few particular callouts:

- Rob Scott – I am delighted to have had your support over the years, and it is great to now have you as part of the Smart WFM team! I appreciate your inputs into this book, in particular the Maximum People Value (MPV) framework.

- Jason Averbook – thank you for your continual words of wisdom, and for supporting HR's evolution.

- Josh Bersin – your yearly wrap on HR tech is something I always look forward to.

- McKinsey, *Harvard Business Review* and the numerous HR publications for the great content continually produced.

The book that has resonated most with me over the last couple of years is *Talent Wins: The New Playbook for Putting People First* by Ram Charan, Dominic Barton and Dennis Carey (Harvard Business Review Press). This book acknowledges talent as the greatest differentiator in an organisation and urges us to manage human capital as wisely as financial capital.

'We must think globally, while acting locally to look after our people and embrace our clients, families, community and environment. This will allow business to reach new heights, increasing value within the workplaces of tomorrow.'

—

Jarrod McGrath

If you've enjoyed reading
The Digital Workforce
you can find out more
about Jarrod McGrath
and Smart WFM on the
following pages.

About Smart WFM

Our Vision

Empower the
workforce now and
into the future

Our Mission

Maximise people
value, productivity
and experience

Our Core Values

- Make a positive social contribution
- Enable a greater sense of purpose for our team
- Make people's lives better
- Harness and share knowledge
- Act with honesty and integrity
- Think from a customer perspective

Who we are

- Industry pioneer
- Easy to work with
- Consulting – advisory
  and implementation
- Business focused
- Product supplier,
  independent
- Built upon experience
  and reputation

How we do it

- Future thinking
- Big picture focus
- Simplified approach
- Strategic alignment and
  partnering
- Proven Smart WFM
  5-Step Methodology
- Embrace digital
- Data-driven decisions
- Measurable value

Working with Smart WFM

Smart WFM is a global human capital management (HCM) consultancy specialising in digital transformation. The company's service offerings include advisory, implementation and support. Smart WFM also offer Service On Demand and the Apitome Software Suite designed to support the HCM customer journey.

Smart WFM have worked with many local and multinational organisations across a variety of industries, including:

St. John of God Healthcare, Austin Health, CBH Group, McCain Foods, Woolworths, National Heavy Vehicle Regulator, Lismore City Council, Northern Beaches Council, Tokyo Electron Singapore, Dominos USA, NTT DATA Business Solutions, EY and UKG

Find out more at:

smartwfm.com

Make the Pledge

Smart WFM is proud of its relationship with Pledge 1%.
We embedded corporate philanthropy into our
business model from inception.

Having a greater sense of purpose to our work
is important to us.

Find out more:

PLEDGE
1%

pledge1percent.org

Supporting the
Indigenous Literacy Foundation
in Australia

Smart WFM is proud to be the ongoing major sponsor of the Australian Business Book Awards, which have raised over $10,000 for the Indigenous Literacy Foundation over two years. Smart WFM is excited to support the great work performed by the ILF around Australia.

The Australian Business Book Awards recognise entrepreneurs, business people and business owners who have written and published a book demonstrating their skill, knowledge and experience in their industry.

Any profits from the Awards are donated to the Indigenous Literacy Foundation, a fantastic organisation doing extraordinary things to raise the level of literacy throughout Indigenous communities.

Are you looking for the perfect gift for your business customers?

If you are looking for the ideal gift for your business customers, Jarrod's latest book is of great value to business owners and managers.

If this sounds like the ideal promotional opportunity for your organisation, contact Smart WFM via:

smartwfm.com